For Morton, posthumously . . . then some valuable forms of experience are doomed to disappearance,

not always to be replaced by something necessarily more valuable than themselves. And this means that

it must always be the case that some values are not compatible, historically compatible, with others, so

that the notion of an order in which all true values are simultaneously present and harmonious with each

other is ruled out, not on the ground of unrealizability due to human weakness or ignorance or other

shortcomings (the overcoming of which could be at least imagined), but owing to the nature of reality itself.

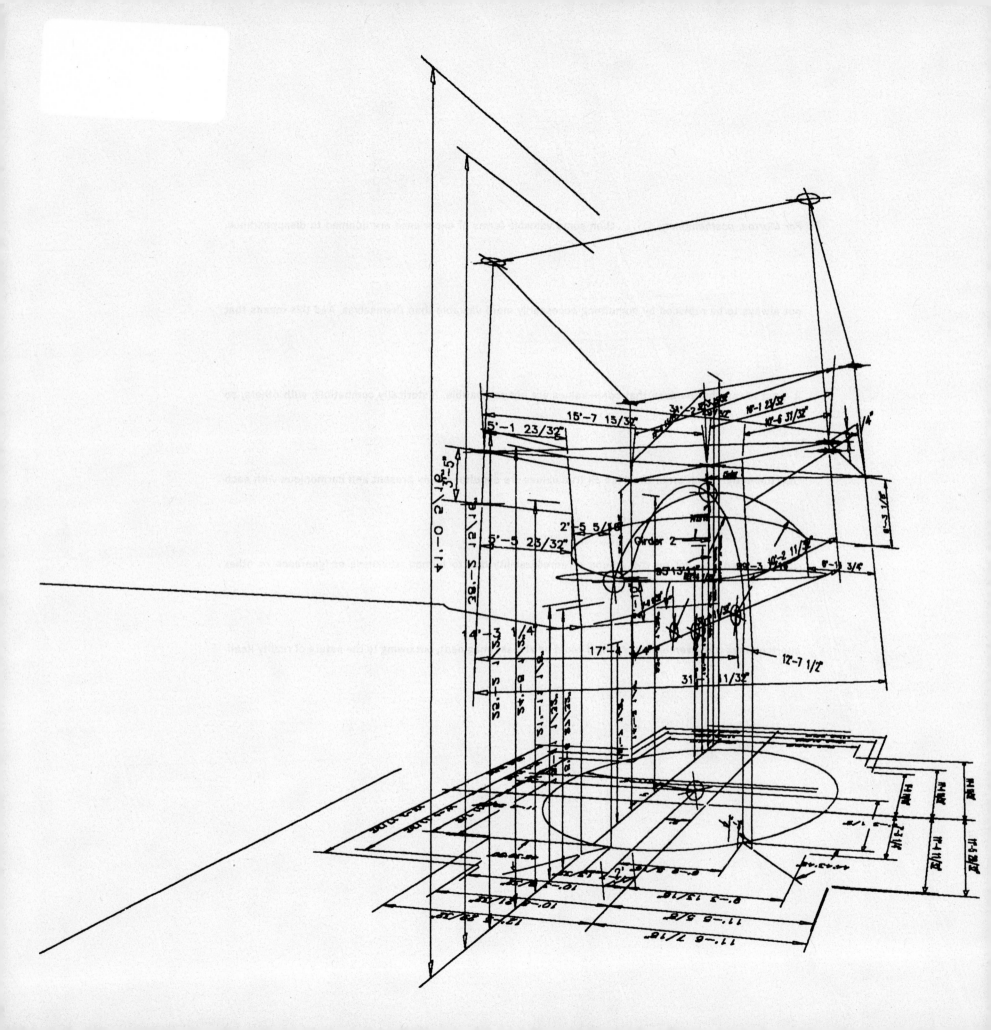

This means that the idea of perfection is ruled out not so much for empirical reasons but because it is conceptually

incoherent, not compatible with what we see history necessarily to be.   Isaiah Berlin, *Against the Current*

Eric Owen Moss THE BOX

edited by Preston Scott Cohen and Brooke Hodge

with an interview by Scott Cohen
photographs by Andrew Bush
and essays by Herbert Muschamp and Peter G. Rowe

Harvard University Graduate School of Design
Princeton Architectural Press

Eric Owen Moss THE BOX

is one of a series of publications of

Harvard University Graduate School of Design

48 Quincy Street

Cambridge, Massachusetts 02138

The catalogue was published in connection with

Eric Owen Moss's appointment as Eliot Noyes Visiting Design Critic in Architecture in the spring of 1993.

International Standard Book Number 1-56898-033-7

Library of Congress Catalog Card Number 94-66961

Published in the United States of America by

Princeton Architectural Press

37 East 7th Street

New York, New York 10003

212.995.9620

Printed in the United States of America

THE BOX *Table of Contents*

Eric Owen Moss's architecture explores the irrational and the agonized. He is attracted to the psychological realm of unresolved and unresolvable problems. He despises the modernist notion of architecture as a scientific solution to well-defined problems. Eric has said, "If someone is simply symmetrical or simply balanced, or simply linear, or simply a narrative, then they are simple-minded. My experience of the world is not that. Sometimes it's hard to believe in the idea of believing." Indeed, it is much too simple to say that Eric Owen Moss's work is merely complicated. The line is simple and the inherent universal order is complex, but not simply for the sake of complexity, nor is it only spatial distortion or manipulation at the expense of orientation and fluidity. When visiting the work one finds an architecture beautifully detailed in crafted spatial sequences, with a surprisingly warm and friendly atmosphere that belies the rather shocking and aggressive nature of the work. Moss's work is, however, without a doubt, an architecture made by someone who is more interested in the questions raised by our culture than in the solutions it offers.

In Eric Moss's work there is an architectural tease, a broken geometry, baroque form and space–his is an architecture that creates a sense of wonder in an otherwise dry and functional environment.

Nowadays questions of architecture–like many other forms of human endeavor–are riddled with a certain modern skepticism or anxiety about our capacities as knowers and, therefore, about our knowledge of the existence and rightness of things, especially in the manner we go about constructing our worlds. Universal design principles, contrary to earlier expectations, can no longer be turned to with any confidence for guidance and support. Modern architecture's alleged promise of a progressive new world did not materialize, and many attempts to organize our urban lives have resulted in technocratic failures, sometimes of monstrous proportions. The skepticism that emerged from these outcomes, while providing a powerful critique of modern circumstances, has done little, however, to relieve our contemporary anxiety about making an architecture of any lasting generality and value.

In the work of Eric Owen Moss we see at least one strong attack or assault on this modern, or one might say now postmodern, condition of skepticism. Passionate and articulate about the role of architects as formgivers and artists, Moss seems to share the view held by Kierkegaard–who he often quotes–that when confronted with something like the idealized edifice of speculative systematic philosophy, individualism and subjective self-commitment are better courses of action. On the other end of the spectrum, far from being numbed into inaction by skeptical critiques of this attitude or that, architectural existence for Moss is a matter of this self-same artistic commitment and of the individual nature of architecture in some essential form as the very basis for gaining and recovering knowledge about its broader possibilities. However, lest the renegade image and confrontational style suggested here be taken too literally, Moss, although clearly in favor of a certain Kierkegaardian individualism, is neither idiosyncratic nor iconoclastic in his architectural viewpoints. His is an affirmative posture and one that is highly involved with each specific project.

The Box, one of several projects completed by Moss in Culver City, California–deep inside the Los Angeles

metropolitan area–aesthetically exemplifies his architectural stance and provides an unusual resolution of at

least some of the problems of both modern universalism and postmodern skepticism raised by the site and

program. At first glance we are presented with a commonplace warehouse structure amid a fragmented and

visually discordant surrounding environment. It is, in fact, typical of much of this area of Los Angeles, where

the very matter-of-fact ordinariness itself begins to undermine a more usual skepticism about the building.

Coming nearer, however, the ordinary, and one might even say universal, image of the warehouse with other

adjacent mechanical structures, quickly evaporates. While unmistakably a warehouse-type structure this is

no ordinary warehouse-type structure, even discounting the odd protrusions above the roofline, which

might otherwise be taken for mechanical equipment.

The box on The Box–the unusual second-story element–on even closer examination and particularly from

below through the skylight–appears like some giant helioscope or similar astronomical instrument atop

the building. Indeed, in some ways this turns out to be not too far from its actual function because of the

eye-like corner window that literally reframes the view of the city like some special optical apparatus.

Furthermore, the way of getting to this privileged vantage point-up stairs and around corners-has an

expressionistic quality, suggesting something of a rehearsal space for the senses, prior to actually taking in the

view, as well as a certain dissociation from the commonplace ground plane below. The architectural

experience-for that is what it is, a palpable experience-ultimately is about the sensation of 'being there' in

the particular milieu of greater Los Angeles, and nowhere else. Moreover, it is neither a contextual response,

which one might expect today from a skeptical, knowing architect building in Culver City, nor in any way

a search for something more universal. It is simply about 'being there.'

Eric Owen Moss has an acute and unfailing sense of making buildings, individually and specifically.

During the Eliot Noyes Lecture he gave at Harvard in 1993, he spent a surprising amount of time on

the details, materials, and technical ways of creating architecture. In this regard, work on The Box

is no exception. On second thought, however, this attention seems to be quite consistent with

the attitude of artistic integrity and individualism associated with Moss. What better way to

affirm the possibility of architecture than by concentrating on the actual making of it? What

better way of avoiding nebulous issues of building in general, let alone systems of materials

and finishes than by emphasizing the very craft of building? As with other aspects of his

extraordinary work, Eric Owen Moss somehow transcends both the universalizing and

skeptical aspects of today's architecture through the sheer individuality, wit, and

appropriateness of his projects.

Scott Cohen INTERVIEWS *Eric Owen Moss*

Eric Owen Moss (top) in interview with Scott Cohen (left), Los Angeles, 1994

Scott Cohen: Today, when we were looking at the railing at the Gary Group building, on the Ince site, it elicited from you a self-critical response. **Eric Owen Moss: I think this has to do with some kind of movement in the work. My response to the railing is a change in emphasis. This is the erogenous handrail. It's not built the way it has to be built so it won't fall down. It's way beyond what is necessary to help somebody get from one level to the next. It gets into how to make things.** You're saying it gets beyond its routine function, and that makes it excessive. Given this criteria, wouldn't you consider most of your work excessive? **The railing drains something from other areas — I'm now changing the focus. I started to feel that these tiny artifacts, not one or two but in the aggregate, dilute the power of the form to yank you around. Maybe the space could stretch you out, or take you somewhere you haven't been, or make something available you didn't know existed. If knowledge is provisional and architecture is contingent on a provisional knowledge, then architecture would move perpetually. Architecture moves by reformulating space. So the formulation of space is the essence of the building. The rail becomes superfluous.** By saying architecture should move, are you suggesting a form of mutation or are you talking about progress? **There's no progress and nobody should be disappointed. You might stand in the same place running or go in circles backwards.** What are those conditions internal to architecture, neither pragmatic nor personal, that thwart your intentions or redirect your predispositions toward a given project? **I don't know. . .it's mutation, thwarting mutation. We never delved into the subject of mutation. I don't know that I've ever felt thwarted, and we've eliminated all of the usual external conditions that everybody bitches about. Sometimes the fight is not with the outside, the fight is with the inside. Be careful when architects whine about politicians and banks and**

Railing detail, Gary Group, Culver City, 1988

clients. It's disingenuous. Architecture is not only the slave of power, or those in power, but it is also about

asserting power. And the power of the architect may be to claim that his frame of reference is the more durable

and his power is the more potent. To make a building in the city, to make the city, is a manifestation of will, a will to power.

A will to form. *Will is formless. Its manifestation is space. So this game is like a contest of power sometimes.*

I think people who are doing architecture don't acknowledge what drives it. Revealing the motivation clarifies

the design act, opens it up overtly: powerful space and spaces as power, both. What if I were to have said,

when we were looking at that point that represents a geometric infinity in your Goalen project, that it was

an example of the sheer phenomenon of an idea encountering material? Why do we always have to make

reference to the architect in the world? Why can't an architectural argument circulate between materials,

forms, and ideas? A geometric ideal has been imposed on steel and the steel is resisting and thickening.

The material will not accept the idea of infinity at that point in your project. Isn't that what it's about? *Well,*

it is about me—in the sense that I decided that that would be the subject of the discussion. It was set up to

raise a question that could only be answered ambiguously. The conclusion was anticipated. It is an idea that has been compromised by

material. *I wouldn't say compromised. A compromise implies that there could be something other than*

Goalen Group, 8522 National Boulevard Complex, Culver City, 1988–90

compromise. There could be a pure answer one way or another. No. It seems that the hypothesis is that the

idea of infinity represented by the intersection of those two geometric entities could be a pure concept, if

it were never physically represented. The material is the proof that once infinity is concretized, it cannot

be. It is begging the question: without concretization, where's architecture? *Didn't you think I knew the*

Conference Room, 8522 National Boulevard, Culver City, 1986–90

constructed ambivalence when I started? Infinity can't be infinity if it's finite. Is that a tautology? You must

have, of course, but what I believe the project asks is, can you build a point, the intersection of two figures?

Can conceptual infinity be sustained by thickness? This is like some of the questions about the birch plywood coming up against the

irregular surface of the wall in the conference room at 8522 National. Yes, infinity, the infinitesimal, the

indeterminately minute dimension. The concept can't be dimensioned. I'm interested in building that dilemma

very precisely and poignantly. I'm not interested in running away from the problem; I'm interested in exposing

the problem—putting its components down. In the end this is not answerable by retreating to literary

generalities on deconstruction. We can't build infinity. Only building demonstrates the split between the

cerebral and the constructed. Goalen suggested infinity, made it tangible. It showed the limits of what you

Detail, Conference Room, 8522 National Boulevard

could build. What you build could suggest what you can't build. The implication is infinity; but you've argued

that this implication is only hypothesized in the personal sense. And this is what I'm questioning. That the

conception of infinity is generic? No, it's not generic. The concept has something of generality in it, but the particular

concrete form in which it has been inscribed has moved it away from that generality. So there is no

architectural generality outside a specific form, generality exists somewhere in the ether? Ether, yes, in the

ether. I agree; that's what I'm arguing for. But architecture has to be more tangible. It's always tangible. So

what I'm saying is, it can be either in the ether and tangible; tangibly in the ether. It seems to me your work

has a great deal to do with the relationship between the tangible and the intelligible world. They suggest one another.

I don't know if they suggest one another so much as they confront one another in your work. I think it's

Scott Cohen INTERVIEWS Eric Owen Moss

more about the oppositions you would like to open up, as opposed to the opposition between conflictual geometries. I think this is a very interesting area of opposition in your work. The opposition between what could be called the ether of the ideal concepts and the material, the concrete. *Let's talk about Mark Rothko as the ether of The Box.*

The architectural equivalent of Rothko couldn't be Mies. I don't know who the architectural equivalent of

Mark Rothko, *Yellow and Gold*, 1956, oil on canvas, 67 1/8 x 62 3/4", The Museum of Modern Art, New York. Gift of Philip Johnson

Rothko would be. Materially, Rothko's very different than Mondrian, for instance. In the ether, they might share strategies, but the tangible is very different. The Box is elemental in a Platonic way. It references something basic, austere. See that Rothko print behind me? The one with the funny colors. The shapes, which are almost precise geometric solids, can be penetrated because of the color—the what's-that-color color. A planar surface that has depth. That's Rothko. You could stick your arm through the color. . . . Like the closet in C.S. Lewis's Narnia. Into the closet and out the other side. It opens out into something else; it's a completely different world nobody anticipated. But not everybody can go there. Only a few. If you're going to stick your arm into that print, you're going to stick your arm right through the wall and it's going to go on, forever. So this is very elemental like The Box. Very elemental and simultaneously goes on forever. To achieve that The Box had to be stripped down. The start of the stripping is getting rid of erogenous handrails. The rails make something where there's really nothing and I think the question for me is how to build nothing, nothing and something. Too much noise; the railing is making too much noise. 'Nothing' always has to do with hypothesized, objective things, like pure geometry. The noise has to do with, let's say, the elemental, the constructed, what I call tectonic. That's what you seem to be saying. *I think I'm equating aspiration to* nothingness in Rothko with the paradox of The Box. The inside and the outside of The Box are the same

material. They are undifferentiated like Plato's cave. You could say that the box is an archetype from tatami

mats to Rothko prints to blocks at Stonehenge. These specific examples approach a general regularity and

order. But when you derive the order mathematically you surrender the architecture. The generic is ethereal,

cerebral. Therefore you have to build it or paint it in a way that makes the cerebral tangible. The antecedent

for The Box is something we know but that doesn't exist physically. There is a further argument, which I reject.

The French playwright Alfred Jarry said: "You won't have destroyed everything until you've destroyed the ruins."

Theater project, Tours

Meaning: make a box in which the box is never recognized. I'm arguing that's too easy. You have to hold onto

the tension between–what is in the ether and in its physicality. An analogous ideal. *Or an analogous space.*

I'm not sure ideal is the right word. Unless there's an alternative ideal, an emotive ideal. The emotive ideal is the material. *And also the form.*

Let's say, to borrow Nietzsche's terms, there's an Apollonian ideal and a Dionysian ideal. So Plato would be

with Apollo in the ether. Rothko would be with Dionysus in the tangible. You have to have both sides. So I'm

arguing for a version of yin and yang that is not static. It's elastic and therefore pieces like the white dot in the

middle of the black might get so big that the black wouldn't be recognized anymore. That's the diagram, a

kinetic elastic diagram. I think The Box and the project for the theater in Tours are getting to something like

that. I want to say something about opposition and reconciliation. I want to pull it together, not only pull it

Theater project, Tours, France, 1993

apart. A lot of the contemporary discussion about prospective directions for architecture has to do with taking sides.

You want a synthetic interaction, not an antithetic dualism. *I want both.* You want an antithetic dualism?

Are you looking for that? *If dualism means a kind of equilibrium is reached, then no.* Equilibrium, as opposed

Aronoff House project, Tarzana, California, 1991

to balance. *An equilibrium, balance. Here's another problem. You can balance on this table in the middle and you can balance on the edge.*

They're both balance of some kind. I would argue for a balance that is precarious, and an equilibrium that is

tenuous, tentative. Okay? Not an equilibrium that is solidified. So I wouldn't argue for standing in the middle

of the table, but I would argue for knowing that the table has a middle, not just an edge. Didn't the equilibrium

in the Aronoff sphere suggest that rolling away could be imminent? *Meaning in architecture is provisional*

so any built equilibrium is also provisional. Equilibrium to disequilibrium and back. Building should be

emotionally kinetic. Prospective movement and prospective movement resisted. Let's distinguish two movements. The movement of the

imagination from the concept of box to the concrete form of this box, and the rolling movement implied by

the Aronoff sphere. The Box isn't saying it's going to fall, or it's going to roll. The Box is saying it's getting

farther from or closer to its concept. *The first movement is a tension, an unresolved tension between what is*

recognizable as a geometric antecedent (the ether) and the demolition of that antecedent (the tangible). The

second is the tension between the object stabilized, completed, and the object in motion, incomplete. Standing

on the horizontal floor plane of The Box confirms both. What's normative in the ethereal box is abnormal for

The Box because the orthogonal moorings, the directions, are gone. It's a box (or is it?) but now what's up?

What's down? What's left? What's right? There's a convention in the ether that is missing physically. And this

Aronoff House project

is the fundamental intention. It's not normal for the box that the floor be where it is. . . *No. The floor, though,*

brings you back to something that is normative; but in the new framework of The Box, the anomaly is the floor.

The Box is a norm in the abstract because we could agree that it represents something that is conventional. We can agree on that, it's not merely personal. *It exists in every building on the street. So it exists, and it exists historically. Okay, so we didn't invent it, for those who feel it must be new and novel. It's original. That The Box has antecedents doesn't preclude its originality. The ethereal box wasn't invented but the tangible manifestation was.* There are two types of tension. One is between the datum and the box. The other is between the intangibility of the box and its emotive, material aspect. *The box in the ether, the box in the world.* I want to ask you about the nature of this encounter. The world and the box remain apart from one another, it seems to me. We know that the floor belongs not to the box but to the world, and we always know what part of the building belongs to the concept "box." There's never any point in the building where either gets caught up in the other such that they reconfigure one another. We are never in neither as a result of their conflict. We know when we're on the staircase, we're in the world; we know when we look at that window in the corner, we're in the box. *You're asking if the building could reinvent the world so we could understand the world differently. The Box has that aspiration. You can't always find the box. You have to locate it in the world. From certain vantage points in the world the physical box and its orthogonal are not apparent. For example, if you're down National Boulevard, you're looking at the stair in an amalgamation with the old warehouse and The Box. A triumvirate, so you don't get it. And while looking at it from underneath or moving up through it you might get lost again.* How about inside The Box itself? When you are in it, it becomes apparent that the walls have been rotated out of the XYZ—they can be returned, by the imagination, to the datum of the world.

Scott Cohen **INTERVIEWS** *Eric Owen Moss*

Not necessarily. You didn't know that the corner points of The Box are referenced at the ends of the steel beams. That brings you back to the generic box. When you're inside, you obviously don't see the external signs. The Box has an internal chronology. You move through it in a designated sequence, no options. The exterior is more variable. To fully understand it one would need to approach from a number of directions simultaneously, including from above

The Box

and below. There's something of a residue of the box when you look up through the glass on the first floor then start up the stair. You see the underside of the stair above. What the hell are these pieces of steel flying around? You can't know. And then you go through a wall to the roof deck under the box but the wall locks out the space you just left. Now more pieces. If you can assemble the pieces in your head maybe now you know. Then, up into The Box and again a different vantage point. You are never physically in a position to unify the disparate pieces (which are not all there anyway). The box can't be understood all at once. *This is a great term, the all-at-once. This is a religious term.* Through experience over time it may be partially understood. *But the pieces of the experience, by intention, are designed to disturb. You don't necessarily know the pieces add up to a total. Perhaps they're not pieces of a whole but pieces of a hole. The box can be looked at as points or as lines, edges, or some combination with some points and some lines missing but not systematically missing. Or it can be understood as a solid or a volume, or a series of planes.* Still, the box and its tangible context are not mutually compromised. *I'm going to turn it around. I'm going to say you're always between the two. You're never totally at one end, and you're never totally at the other end. You're always somewhere in the middle. Even*

The Box, under construction, 1993

if you're aspiring to one end. . . In the middle doesn't preclude discussing the ends. *No.* The pure concept of

the box is never interfered with, it's never undone. There's not a point at which the box is erased or deflected. *I mean, would this be an argument for erasing more of the physical residue of the box?* No I'm not only saying erase. I'm saying the lineaments of the box need to be partly deformed, by the encounter with the world. On purely geometric terms, I think the problem is that the box remains too indifferent to the datums of the world passing through it. Where is the work on their conflict being done? Do you think the project overcomes a bilateral dialectic between paradigms? The floor refers to the world, the walls refer to the box? Does it get beyond that? *There's an aspiration for reconciliation.* I'm looking for reconciliation. Where's the reconciliation? *If the box were first and the floor were second, then the form of the floor as a plan is a consequence of the position of the box.* The consequence is an intersection. *There was a possibility at one point that The Box wouldn't be inhabited. That seemed to dilute its meaning. But it was discussed. There is a certain tension between the question of occupancy, the position of the wall, and the form of the floor. The floor is not orthogonal. In terms of its edges, it's all over the place.* But the floor remains a true horizontal. It does not concede to the box. You don't want to say they intersect each other; that's what I would say. The horizontal plane intersects the box and together they generate a third lineament, which is the line of intersection between them. Is intersection a reconciliation? *They're not simply intersecting. They are both adjusted. The floor has made concessions to the inclination of the walls and the inclination in the walls has made concessions to the presence of the inhabited floor. The position of the box relates to the prospect of being inside it.* I'm saying that the geometry of the box and the floor need to merge as opposed to intersect. Merge or mutate.

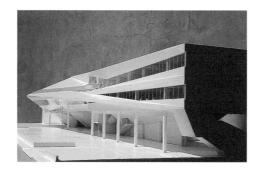

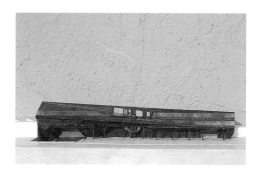

Can you tell me what it should be conceptually? At least hypothetically. It's an interesting question. If there are

Hercules project, Hayden Tract, Culver City, 1992

aspects of the problem that exist as identities, then the question is could they share a third identity? That's

Hercules project

right. I think that the concept box is not likely to produce a third term because it forces one into the idea

of a dualistic intersection, as opposed to a synthetic transformation. I'm not sure it's able to converge with

something. In a different way, the Aronoff sphere can't either. I think the project that investigates

conceptual deformation is Hercules. The Hercules project does not possess only a pure geometric identity.

It almost does. It's a different step. It actually works like this: the building is 316 feet long. At one end is a figure

that is three-sided. You don't quite see it. The other end has four sides. There is a transformation from a four-

sided figure to one that is three-sided. In the Hercules building you never step into the same form twice. The

Box and the Aronoff sphere maintain their opposites. They're more Platonic. Hercules is your Dionysus.

Doesn't the box, in advance, preclude transformation as a subject, by forcing discrete pieces into a dualism,

into the idea of intersection? *Tension in the box is between recognizing it as a box and not. And the problem of inhabiting The Box is secondary*

Yes, that's how I see it. *You're saying the floor, the stairs are secondary. The question is, could they be*

primary? The force of the box—and the problem of inhabiting the building could produce a conceptual equity

in opposition or in reconciliation. I would say, how can we turn the floor into something conceptual?

Something as conceptual as the box? I think the opposition between the function of the floor, and the box

as a concept, maintaining that dialectic, doesn't help. I think the argument you set up in Hercules is

different. It has two dialectics. Not only does it address the opposition between geometry and inhabitation,

Scott Cohen **INTERVIEWS** *Eric Owen Moss*

it also investigates the opposition between two figures and their transformation *through* one another, *into* one another. **Let me ask you something. What you're arguing is that architecture is contaminated by the problem of inhabiting?** Exactly. Exactly. Or contaminated by materials. For example, like when you attempt to concretize an infinity in the Goalen project. Contamination, if you will, is the commencement of architecture. **And the question is whether you could pull out of the issue of inhabiting as a conceptual issue. . .** That would be on par with . . . . . . *would get an equity position in the language of First Interstate Bank. . .* Thank you. **With the ethereal box contra the tangible box.** Exactly. **This is where we were at the beginning. The first meaning of architecture has nothing to do with use or the problem of inhabiting. It's about somebody's will to power. Will is the requisite component to give it a presence.** Let's go back to painting. I'm just going to make an analogy; see if it's useful to you. Jackson Pollock could be said to have narrowed the space for exploring the relationship between the act of painting and the representational and the objective status of paint. Let's say he has accomplished this by making radical reductions that move painting away from certain conventions. Pollock. He has narrowed the scope. Then someone like Gerhard Richter comes along. He continues the exploration of painting, the act of painting, painting with paint that represents paint. Instead of flinging paint, Richter uses a trowel. He scrapes the paint in a way that makes it impossible to identify the means by which it was applied. Pollock reconfigures the process of applying paint; Richter confounds it. The question for me is this: could such a radical reduction occur in architecture? Is there a way to construct such a narrow space for investigation in architecture? **Pollock did something that's of interest in terms of your question, which has to do with narrowing the field.**

When you narrow the field, you're trying to broaden the field. You're trying to make it about nothing, which is everything. Okay? Which is part of the problem of trying to express by implication something you can't reach. It's an aspiration. You're talking about issues of content related to issues of technique. In this case, technique means no brushes, one color—or even less than one color (meaning the color is not recognizable in a conventional spectrum of colors). The question of what Pollock did in your paradigm is about elimination of the superfluous while extending the contents. I think he only narrowed it. And I'm not sure he narrowed it to broaden it. I'm not sure where the Apollonian side is in Pollock's painting. There is a cerebral box and a tangible box. They implicate each other.

What implicates Pollock's paint? In Pollock's work if one looked at the paintings and knew that paint was flung, one could imagine the throwing distance. One could imagine all sorts of other things that are implied by the configuration of the paint. ***That's the Dionysian side; what's the Apollonian side? The rectangular form***

Gerhard Richter, *793-3 Green/Blue*, 1993, oil on canvas, 94 1/2 x 94 1/2", Courtesy Marian Goodman Gallery, New York

of the canvas? The form of the canvas is one and the other is when there are black streaks or other colors over and under white streaks, simultaneously. ***A form for a sequence of applying color and how one stacks things—*** Yes. Stacking. Framing. Those are Apollonian. ***The problem with using the form of the canvas argument is that it's so generic. Every artist could argue the Apollonian shape of his canvas.*** And the horizontal floor is too generic for the architect. ***I'm talking about the box in the ether. The floor is another question. And an interesting question. The concept of the box has no analogy in Pollock's painting.*** So Pollock gets rid of the brush. What's your architectural equivalent? ***There is no roof and no wall and no floor. No material distinctions. All the same cement plaster. The roof is the wall is the floor. No tradition of roof, no copper***

gutters. Seamless. It's a roof because it happens to be on top. So you're erasing conventional distinctions

by confirming the box instead of the sky. *Jackson Pollock told us the traditions in painting, in coloration, in*

Jackson Pollock, *One (Number 31, 1950)*, 1950, oil and enamel on unprimed canvas, 8'10" x 17' 5 5/8", The Museum of Modern Art, New York. Sidney and Harriet Janis Collection Fund (by exchange)

perspective, in terms of technique were no more useful than what he wanted to put down. Like Joyce. Can't

write a sentence that starts with a capital letter, has a noun, a verb, and a period. No good. So when I write a

sentence there are antecedents that everybody knows to measure Joyce. And there are antecedents for

Jackson Pollock; you walk in a museum, you see the next guy who did it differently. For architecture to confront

both the old problem and the new problem, and a new recitation of a provisional solution to the new problem

which is the old problem, I'm not going to make room to face the rain god of the Yucatan the way Professor

Lampugnani wants it on the banks of the Main.[1] So you've undone the relationship of roofs and walls, but so

1 The reference here is to a January 1994 article in *Der Spiegel* by Vittorio Magnago Lampugnani, a former director of the German Architecture Museum,

has Frank Gehry, so has Peter Eisenman, so have a lot of people. What have you, Eric Owen Moss, done?

in which he advocates a return to traditional nineteenth-century architecture and a repression of experimentation as an antidote for what ails modern cities.

Look at the difference between Rothko and Pollock; it's very useful because they don't introduce

provisionality in the same manner. *Right.* In other words, what particular, specific way do you do it that is

distinct and personal? You talk about personal, I want to get to it. You're talking about a general concept;

a relationship between roof and wall that is well understood by many of your contemporaries. *The discussion could exist generally and*

could be understood generally, so there's some shared ground. There's a fundamental difference in terms of

the question of one's own originality and the relationship of originality to history. For instance, The Box is really

a traditional building. The modern conception of architecture is formed. Time moves forward, progress is

forward. Science is forward. And architecture must be forward. The architects you mention know only forward.

Scott Cohen INTERVIEWS *Eric Owen Moss*

I was reading something out of a diary of Kierkegaard the other night, and he said if you work hard enough you can be your own father. And everybody who makes something wants to be his own father—the origin. You want to deny that what you do has a source external to you. And I'm not denying it. Lampugnani's vanity is confirmed by claiming that the pedigree of antecedents is the history of building. This is where he makes his discovery. The guys who are part of the residue of the Enlightenment think that the way to go forward is to cut yourself off from whatever preceded you. That makes you a hero. This only makes you simple-minded. If I could deliver both forward and backward in a building that would be a difference. I would say that, finally, it is the retention of ideal geometry that distinguishes your work from some of your contemporaries, with whom you nevertheless share some interest in the fragmentary, the multiplicitous, and the indeterminate. *Yes, I think that's true. And this is what contributes to the sensation that one is experiencing something coherent, against the idea of its fragmentary quality. That's right. There's something set up against it, so there's the prospect of coherence. It is like the guy waiting in front of Kafka's door. You know, the door of the law. The guard closes the door, the man dies, and the light shines from under the door. The possibility of building the sensibility of that parable.* It is about the paradigm remaining on the horizon. It is about the possibility of coming up against that door and pressing on it. That's why I wanted to hone in on the question of geometry. Because when you get to the questions of so-called experience, you cannot be sufficiently specific. I think the idea has to do with the relationship between ideal geometry and the indeterminate release of oppositions. *I'm trying to figure out what bothers me about that.* I know it bothers you. *It bothers me because if you've explained it then I'm done. There should be a tension in the work. I didn't want you to know what's coming next. I didn't want to be a predictable conceptual model or a saleable product. You want to buy that? Call Eric. And he'll give you one of those . . . And if somebody thinks that there's a certain amount of importance or prestige associated with that body of imagery, they'll come and buy it. At that point it loses its investigatory aspect; it arrives at an end.* The problem is imagery, exactly. Imagery as opposed to geometry. *I think that we're going to come back to the ideal geometry. Wasn't all convention once unconvention? Convention equals unconvention plus time, that's all. I don't want to stop moving. I don't want to go around looking for a signature. All I'm saying is your ideal geometry and the indeterminate release of oppositions should be provisional.* I understand. But could we say that what you want to avoid is the image that overtakes the provisional, makes itself known and static? Ideal geometry kept on the horizon creates a possibility that isn't a signature because it's provisional in its essence. Is that a possibility? *Yes, because it doesn't reside, finally, in the tangible, or in the image. But it does reside in the aspiration to move toward the unreachable. And therefore the work should continue to express that ambivalence. It should always express the light under the door, as well as the inability to go through it, okay?* That's what the infinity detail does. The ideal makes the aspiration tangible. *And I think you're right about that. I remember talking to Gehry about the way he works, and I remember him making the argument that the mechanism is infinitely variable. And therefore there are all sorts of possibilities inherent, and you never get to the end of it. I think the aspiration to an ideal, which is embodied in something Euclidian could also operate that way. The possibilities are limitless as long as you remember that it's an aspiration, and not for Madison Avenue. It's not a marketable, recognizable image, you know?*

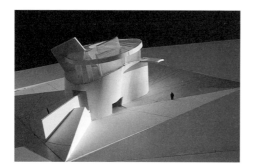

How important is it that you deal with different geometries? Why don't you make ten sphere projects? The aspiration is one thing, the specific choice of geometry is another. *Or, why isn't it always the box?* The

The Squish, (Sun Foundation project), Santa Fe, New Mexico, 1991

sphere, by not containing the orthogonal, confounds the floors, walls, roofs differently than the rotated box. *No question.* The rotation of the box implies a movement that the sphere never needs to imply. *No question.* A sphere is more radical. I think the Aronoff sphere is a more daring deployment. *Is that a virtue?* It might be. *More daring is better than less daring?* Well I think it is. *I agree with you; I'm just not sure that the sphere is the embodiment of more daring. Perhaps we should be talking about the project for the artist, Janet Saad-Cook, at the Very Large Array in New Mexico.* Yes, I know what you're talking about. Warped surfaces. *I call it a squish. The squish operates differently than the sphere although the circle is common to both. The sphere has an unequivocal reference between center and edge. There's a point in the center to which every point on the perimeter has an inexorable association. The box doesn't have that strength. The geometric center of the box is not so compelling. The sphere has a different kind of association between its surface and its inside. It's more obligatory.* More all at once. *Yes.* Hercules and the Squish are not a version of a paradigm that is recognizable; they transform their paradigms by means of deformation, primarily, and concretization, secondarily. Aronoff remains a version of a sphere. *Are you saying that the sphere is a paradigm?* Yes, the sphere is a paradigm. *No, the sphere is not a paradigm. The paradigm is the operation on the sphere.* I'm calling the operation a process of transformation and deformation. The

The Squish

sphere doesn't get squashed; the box doesn't get inflected. *No.* But in Hercules and in the Squish project in New Mexico, they do. The form doesn't exist ipso facto. In Hercules, you've got a triangle, you've got a

Scott Cohen **INTERVIEWS** *Eric Owen Moss*

square. Those two planes undergo a deformative process, I would argue, in a way that Aronoff and The Box

do not, even though they are partially erased. I wouldn't call erasure a process of deformation. *Hercules holds onto both ends,*

both ideals, but it is almost a middle. But the Squish doesn't have the ideal ends that Hercules has. Hercules

has the four-sided, it had the three-sided and the in-between. The Squish is only about the middle; Hercules is

about the middle and the ends; and The Box is only about the ends, the corners. The Aronoff sphere is only

about the end. What's interesting about the Squish is the memory of the cylinder, which makes the action

of the squish legible. *There is a plane where the actual plan profile of the cylinder exists.* Let me ask you,

what is the implication of the difference between the squishing of a cylinder and the intrusive carving of

the sphere? *There's an obvious difference; it has to do with camouflaging the aspiration, or even denying it. I*

might get to a point where there is no more aspiration. All right? Instead, there is a kind of cynicism . . . an act

of cynicism. In other words, The Box has a positivist sense, or an optimistic aspect. But in the Squish the

tangible manifestation of the ethereal ideal is gone. Unlike the tangible box, in the Squish the cylinder hardly exists. No ends?

No center? *There actually is still a piece. Very delicate but poignant.* The memory of a cylinder is there. *It's*

hard to find. It's very hard to find. That's the issue; it's not hard to find in The Box. *No. And it's not even hard*

to find in Hercules, but harder. So if you were looking for a line of progression, it's starting to look like those

literal associations with the aspiration might disappear. You could probably go for a long ride on that cynicism.

I mean the motion of the project, the idea of no ideal. But it doesn't let go of its ideal. It lets go of its explicit

physical presence, partial or whole. *There's of course another argument, which is Plato's. The ideal is manifest as the real.*

The ideal as distinct isn't needed. But in architectural terms, I think the question is whether you need the psychological association. Does it have to be there? What is the meaning of the disappearance? I'm raising the question of the different actions taken to decompose or deform what you called physiognomic memory or aspiration. *The way the Aronoff sphere evolves, how it moves from a pure soccer ball to what it is, holds the aspiration. Okay? Whereas the act of the squish in the most fundamental way contests the physical presence of the aspiration.* The physical presence must be there for you. *I'm not saying that. I'm just thinking about it.* Saying it is in your work. *I'm saying it seems to be varying.* But that has to do with being able to account for your buildings—the tangible and the intelligible aspects being the arena where the opposition gets played out. That's what it means to me. *I agree with you. What I meant by cynical was the physical abandonment of an ideal. I would say that Coop Himmelblau's stuff from a long distance might mean precisely that.* Could be perceived as gratuity. *Might—and it's not. If Wolf said to me, "Helmut and I got drunk and we closed our eyes and made a drawing without looking. And this drawing was the basis for several projects," so this is not a gratuitous remark; it has a lot of meaning. I'm saying very consciously that my work is quite different.* It certainly is. It gets away from the personal. *I wouldn't want to argue that it's impersonal. But it suggests something that is both personal and suprapersonal.* Exactly, suprapersonal. *Okay? But it is not supra-nothing.* Not transcendental, either. *No.* Okay. Thank you for the suprapersonal personal category. Maybe that's what we were looking for. *Supra.*

Scott Cohen INTERVIEWS *Eric Owen Moss*

THE BOX *photographs by Andrew Bush*

Today, when the issue of survival comes up in architecture, the subject is usually "sustainable" design: a framework for restraining buildings and their inhabitants from further degrading the physical environment. But survival should be staked to the mental as well as the material life of buildings. Life depends on designs that reflect or reform relationships in consciousness. The mind needs a body to dwell in, but it also requires life supports of its own. Without them, the body may well lapse into a coma.

In Culver City, a group of industrial buildings has survived because Eric Moss has rewired their inner life. Retooling their workings, he has enabled these aging structures to attract a new kind of tenant, filling the void left by the erosion of the manufacturing base that initially brought them into being. These projects could only have occurred at the dawn of genetic engineering. They are mutated buildings for a mutated city. We can talk about them as works of art, but they are also strategies for survival. For me, they illustrate how art can reinforce endurance in environments where change is a reliable constant.

I had a date with Eric Moss in January 1994—the morning the big earthquake struck Los Angeles. Thrown out of bed at 4:30 in the morning, I stood on the sidewalk outside my hotel, watching dawn come up on a city in shock. Moss was supposed to pick me up at nine, and to my relief he pulled up right on time. I shouldn't have been surprised, because the episode was not unlike Moss's architecture. Walls fly away, ceilings disappear, stairs perform daredevil leaps across heart-stopping voids, but in the end a design prevails: a connection is made across space and time. Things fall apart, but the center somehow holds.

We were going to look at The Box, the most recent of Moss's Culver City projects. Moss was wearing dark glasses and

an air of unflappable cool as we drove from Santa Monica to Culver City. His message, not all that understated, was:

this happens here all the time. Stop acting like a tourist. I said, Oh? When was the last time the freeway fell down

in three pieces? Moss couldn't, come to think of it, remember a time when a quake had taken out the freeway.

Still, as we peered through the windshield, I began to understand why Moss could regard the morning's upheaval

as a common occurrence: even on days without seismic disturbance, the city inhabits a more or less steady

state of spatial, visual, and social shocks. The quake's visible effects–disordered little piles of brick on the

sidewalk, cracks in tiled walls–these were nothing compared to the vast disruption that is the city itself.

The freeway broken into pieces is no more violent than the freeway intact, pounding out its lyrical, brutal

logic of disconnection over the city it ostensibly knits together. The place expands and contracts under

the pressure of its simultaneous desire to become a city and to escape one.

"The Box" is a charged term in American architectural history. The most celebrated act of our most

celebrated architect, Frank Lloyd Wright, was the destruction of the box. With the open floor plan,

the corner window, the berm wall, and the car port, Wright broke down conventions of enclosure

and exclusion to create the classic suburban prototype. Rooted in a vision of the future in which

the city had dispersed into the countryside, the prairie house sought a new equilibrium

between the individual building and shared social space.

Moss's Box readjusts the equilibrium to suit conditions a hundred years down the road. For the future has not turned out exactly as Wright had hoped. Urban dispersal is a reality, but it has not resulted in the integration of architecture with the land. Instead, buildings have become the land, or have artificially conditioned it into a building material. Rather than provide the connective tissue between buildings, the land has enabled buildings to be disconnected from each other, a series of boxes, strung out in disarray.

Still, if you survey the city from a certain angle and a certain speed, an urban image does cohere. In a city where virtually all architecture occupies the foreground, the senses register the city as a series of leaps from form to form, color to color, sign to sign, the whole tenuously held together by the framing device of the windshield and by the speed at which the frame devours the images passing through it. The question is, how to keep that angle of vision, how to maintain the speed? How to make buildings that are not like cars stuck in traffic, buildings that are not dull, disappointing let-downs after the vision that discloses itself through the frame?

That is the question to which Moss's Culver City buildings have supplied a series of stunning answers. The stunts they perform mirror the tricks that the city plays upon the eyes of those moving through the city. He has recreated "the box" not to destroy it one more time but to teach it poise. A sense of balance has grown stronger because of the challenge the design has inflicted upon it. Kenneth Tynan famously wrote that what, when drunk, one sees in other women, one sees in Garbo sober. What, when driving, one sees in Los Angeles, one sees in Moss on foot.

Eric Moss's buildings do not feel the way they photograph. Pictures emphasize their formal idiosyncrasies. They are real enough, but what you feel when you are inside the buildings is the powerful sense of logic governing their relationship to the city outside. Their idiosyncrasies are part of that relationship. They establish that a subjective mind is at work, constructing a set of places that recalls the process of their creation. But to see them in context is to appreciate the degree to which that subjectivity functions as an objective mode of expression. The city around them is a repertory of little pieces that spire to some kind of objective norm–to history, technology, structure, standardization, not to mention all the echoes of the 19th century codes for domesticity, government power, culture, religion, and industry. But the collective result of all this yearning for normativity is a richly textured urban fabric of big, little, and medium-sized subjectivisms. Each bid for order only adds to the babble it strains to shut out.

Architecture, in such a place, cannot attain an objective frame of reference by reproducing older norms or inventing new ones. It can, however, frame the city's subjective texture as a close approximation of objective truth. This is what Eric Moss's buildings accomplish. Revealing the city's logic by turning it outside-in, Moss readjusts the world of material reality by reaching down hungrily into the mind.

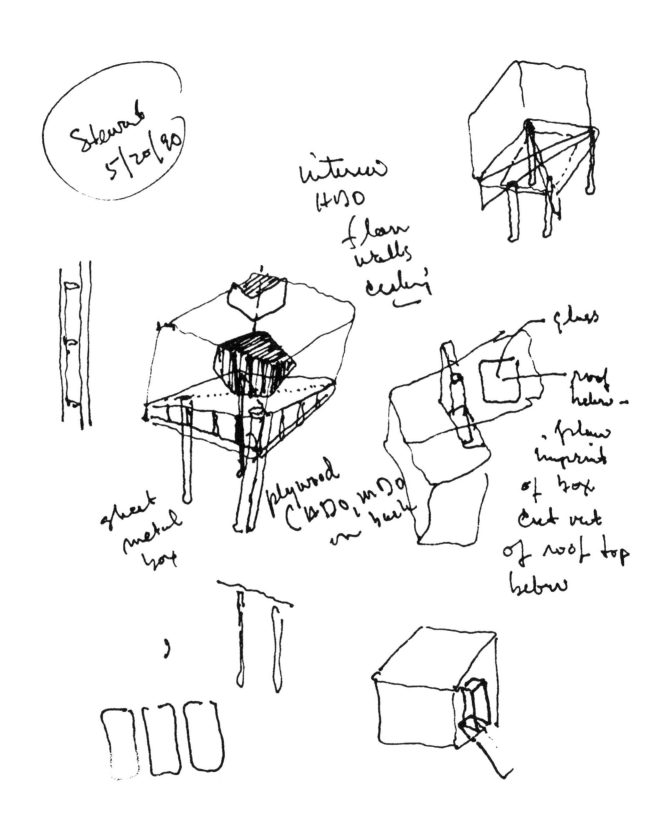

Stewart
5/20/90

interior
H_2O
floor
walls
ceiling

glass

roof below —

filow imprint
of box
cut out
of roof top
below

plywood
$CaDO_i mDO$
on black

sheet
metal
box

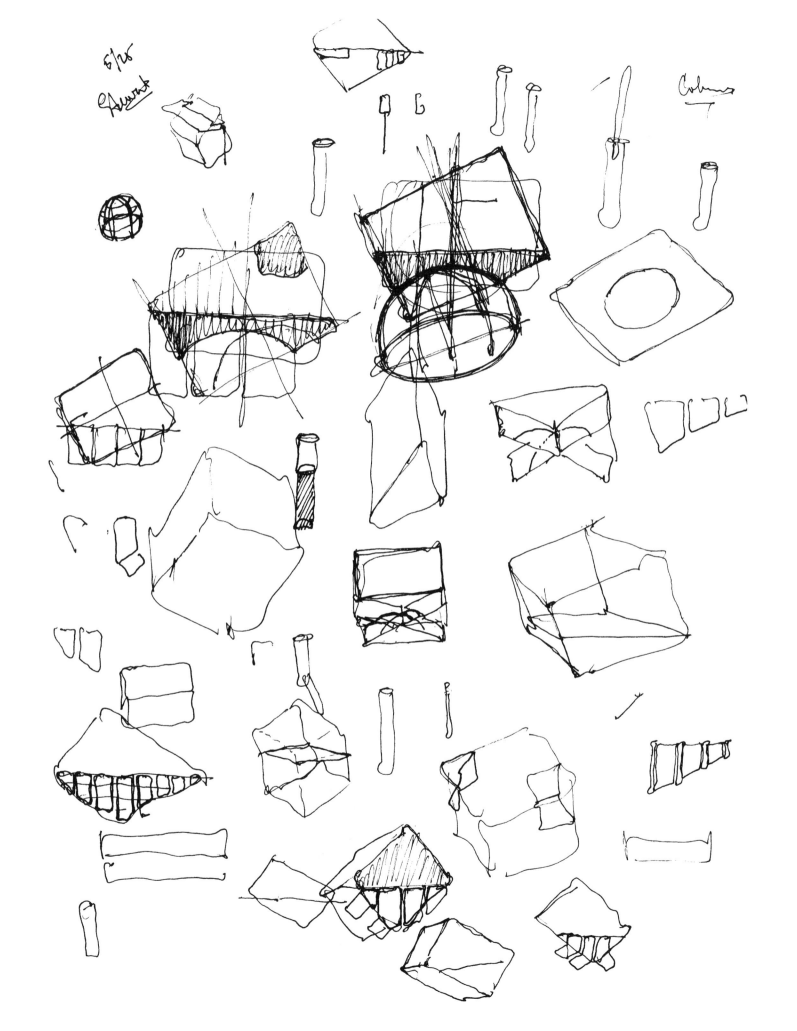

Gary Stamp

- Sheet metal @ ducts
  seams
- ABS · lamps

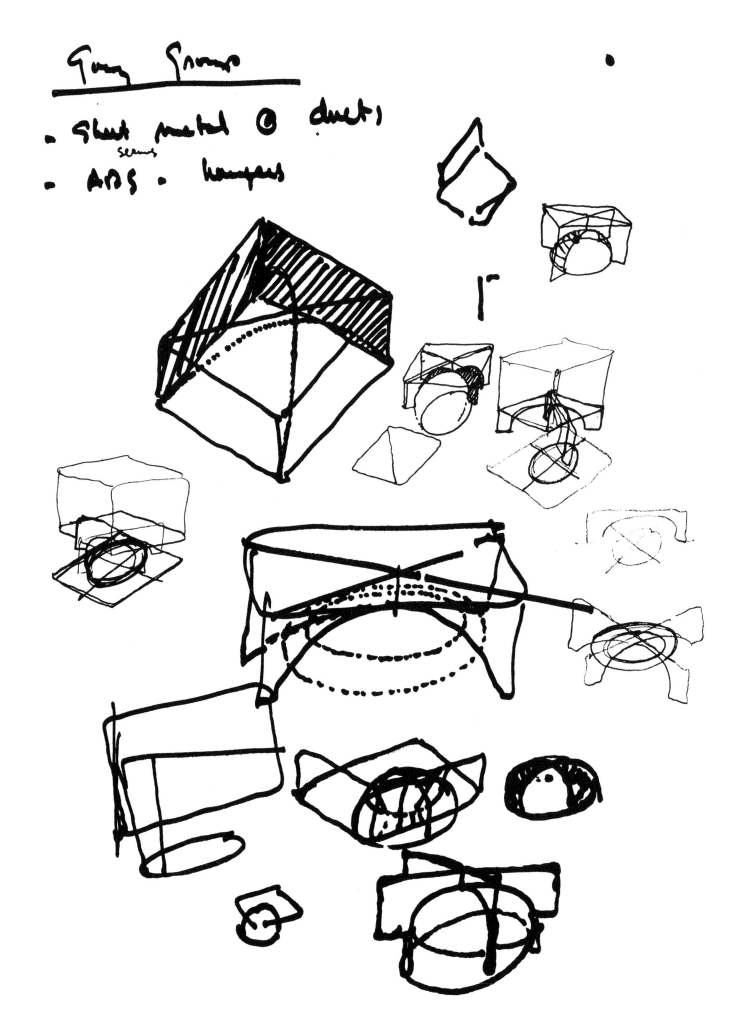

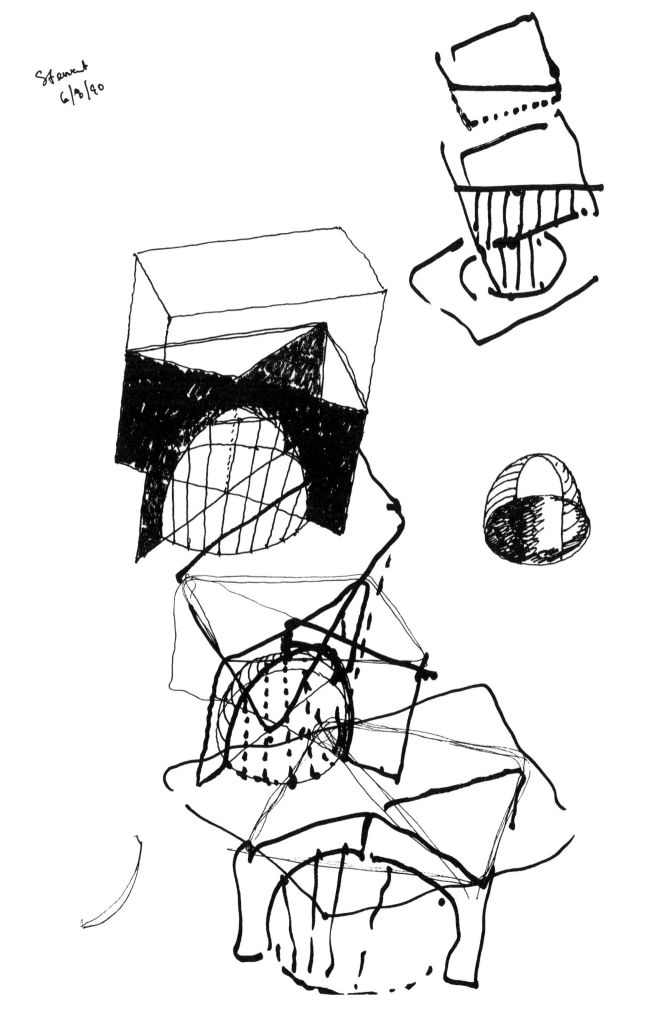

Stewart
6/8/90

Stewart
6/20/90

- yellow wall
  perforated over
  galvanized studs
- corner windows; frame
  · glass
- HVAC corner
- HVAC @ interior
- cloth @ hyperbolic stair
- cloth @ cylinder
- cylinder + piers

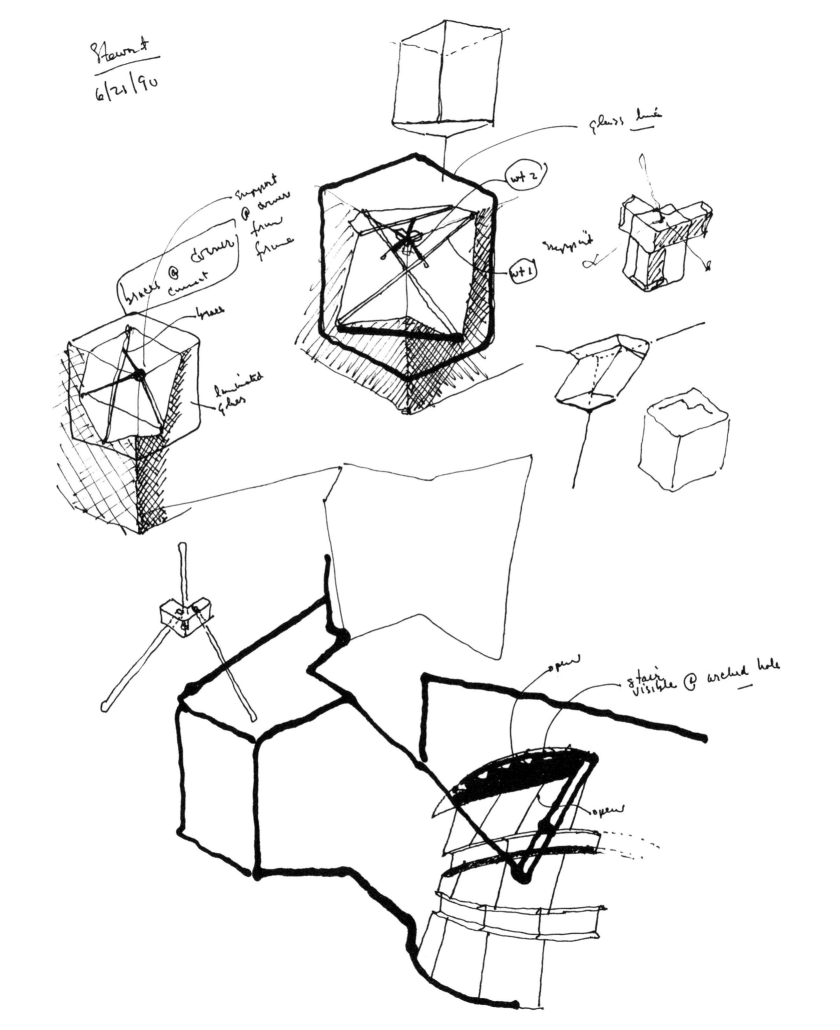

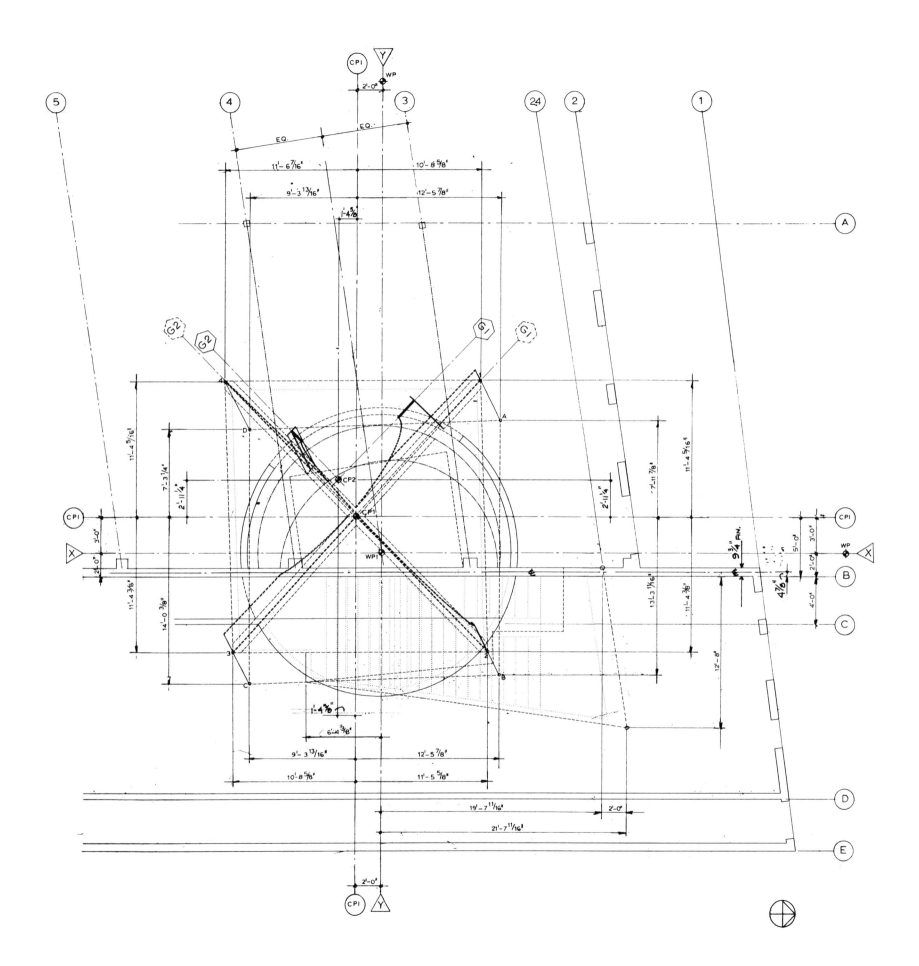

CONSTRUCTION DOCUMENT *Control Plan* SCALE 1/8"=1-0'

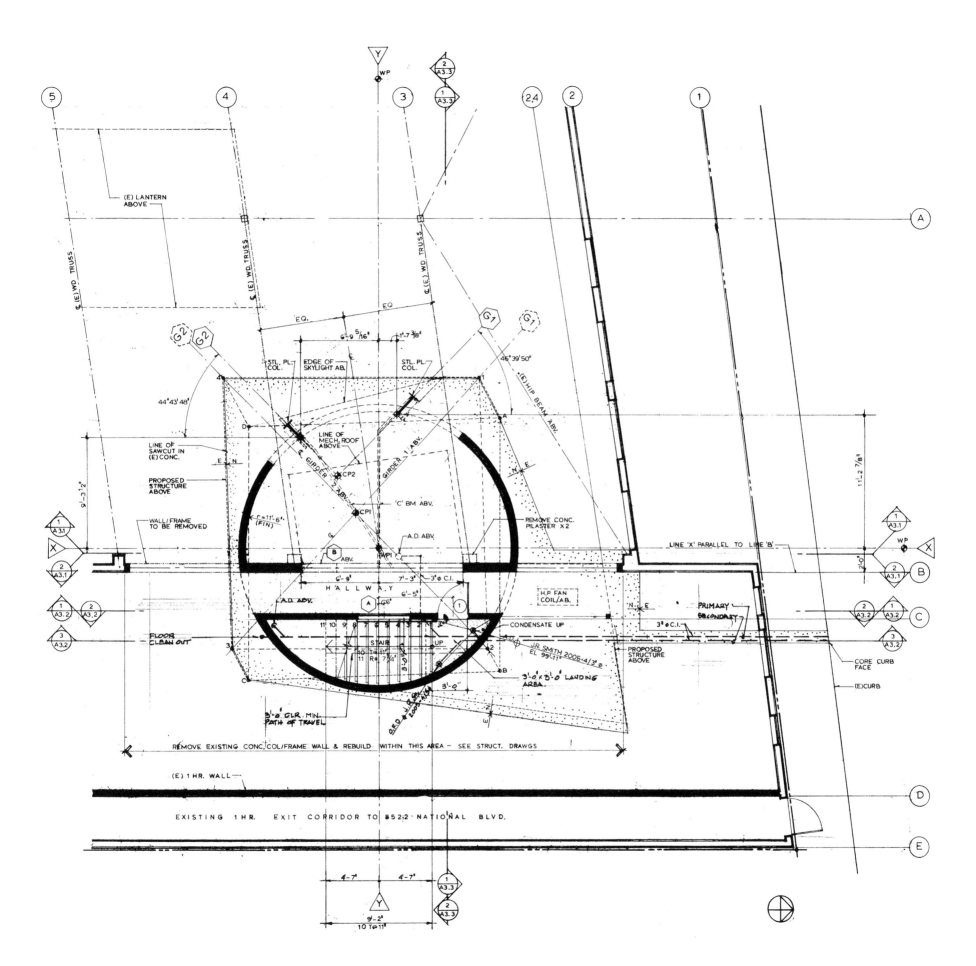

CONSTRUCTION DOCUMENT *Ground Floor Plan* 0'-0" SCALE 1/8"=1-0'

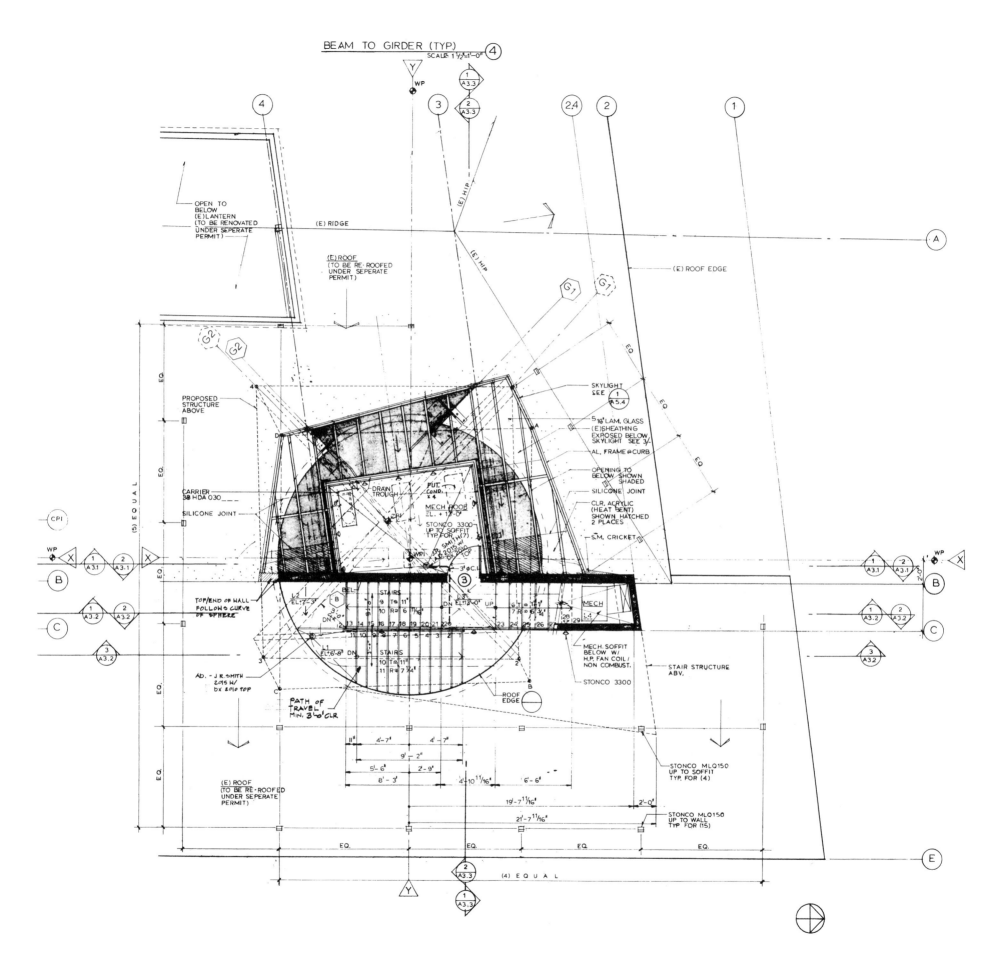

BEAM TO GIRDER (TYP)
SCALE 1½"=1'-0"

OPEN TO BELOW
(E) LANTERN
(TO BE RENOVATED UNDER SEPERATE PERMIT)

(E) RIDGE

(E) ROOF
(TO BE RE-ROOFED UNDER SEPERATE PERMIT)

(E) ROOF EDGE

PROPOSED STRUCTURE ABOVE

SKYLIGHT SEE 3/22

5/16" LAM. GLASS
(E) SHEATHING EXPOSED BELOW SKYLIGHT SEE 3/

AL. FRAME @ CURB

CARRIER 38 HDA 030

SILICONE JOINT

DRAIN TROUGH

PUT. COND. x 4

OPENING TO BELOW SHOWN SHADED

SILICONE JOINT

MECH ROOF
EL. + 17'-0"

STONCO 3300 UP TO SOFFIT TYP. FOR (7)

CLR. ACRYLIC (HEAT BENT) SHOWN HATCHED 2 PLACES

S.M. CRICKET

TOP/END OF WALL FOLLOWS CURVE OF SPHERE

BEL. STAIRS
EL. 7'-3"

9 T@ 11"
10 R@ 6 11/16"

DN EL. 13'-0" UP

6 T@ 11"
7 R@ 6 3/4"

MECH

MECH. SOFFIT BELOW W/ H.P. FAN COIL/ NON COMBUST.

STAIR STRUCTURE ABV.

AB. - J.R. SMITH 2015 W/ DX 2010 TOP

STAIRS
EL. 6'-8" DN

10 T@ 11"
11 R@ 7 3/4"

STONCO 3300

PATH OF TRAVEL MIN. 3'-0" CLR.

ROOF EDGE

(E) ROOF
(TO BE RE-ROOFED UNDER SEPERATE PERMIT)

11"   4'-7"   4'-7"
9'-2"
5'-6"   2'-9"
8'-3"   4'-10 11/16"   6'-6"

19'-7 11/16"   2'-0"

21'-7 11/16"

STONCO MLQ150 UP TO SOFFIT TYP. FOR (4)

STONCO MLQ150 UP TO WALL TYP FOR (15)

EQ.   EQ.   EQ.   EQ.

(4) EQUAL

CONSTRUCTION DOCUMENT *Mechanical Roof Plan* 13'-0" SCALE 1/8"=1'-0'

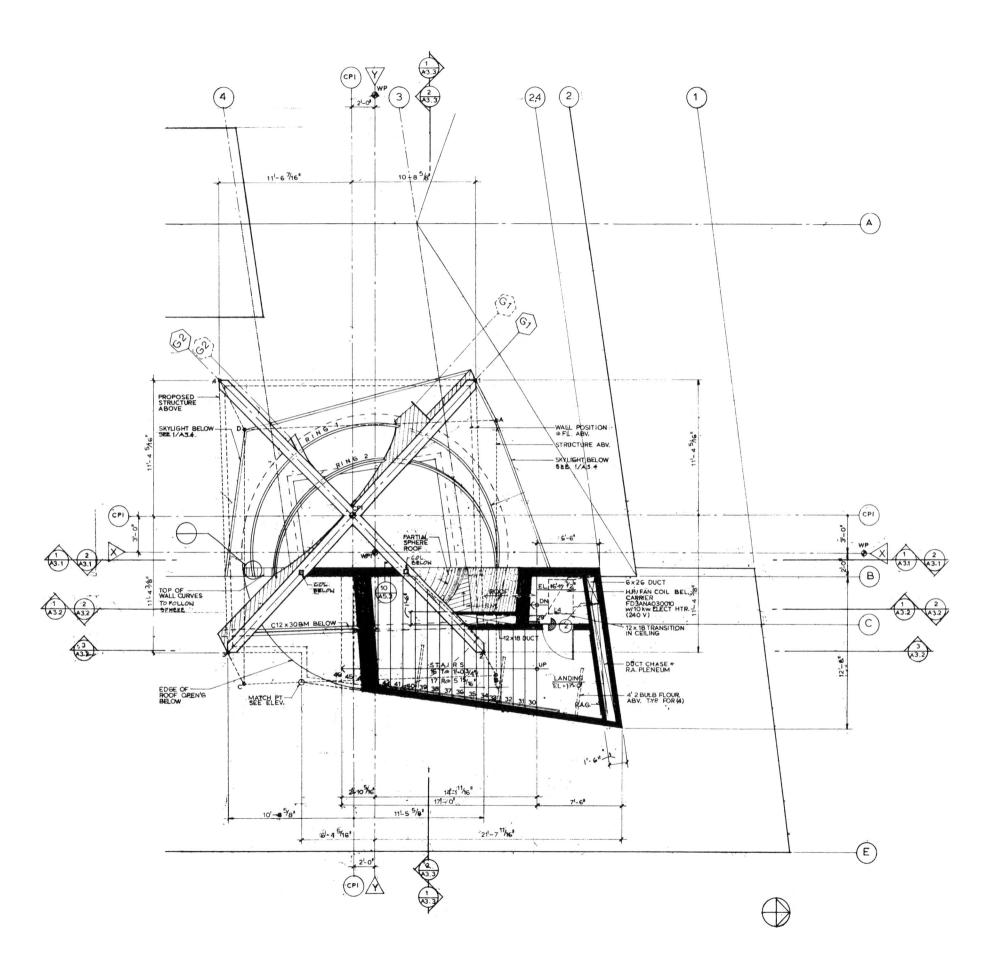

CONSTRUCTION DOCUMENT *Floor Plan @ T. O. Girder* 25'-2 1/2" SCALE 1/8"=1-0'

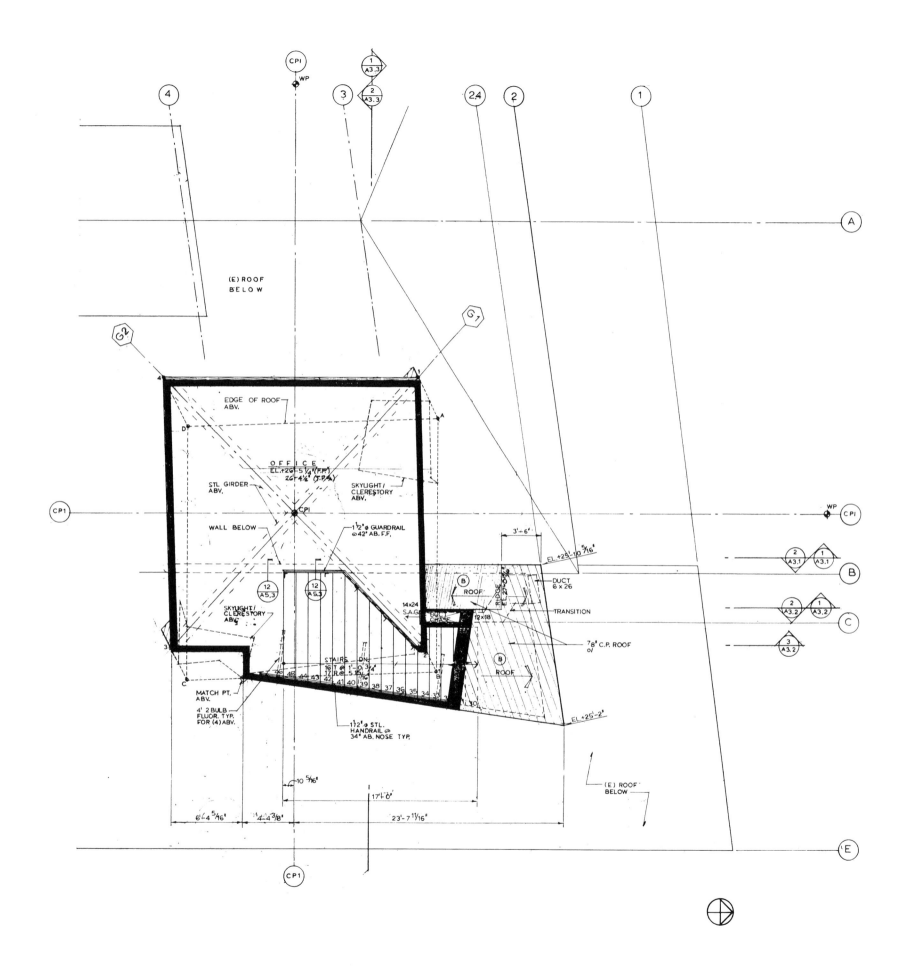

CONSTRUCTION DOCUMENT *Second Floor Plan* 26'- 4 1/2" SCALE 1/8"=1-0'

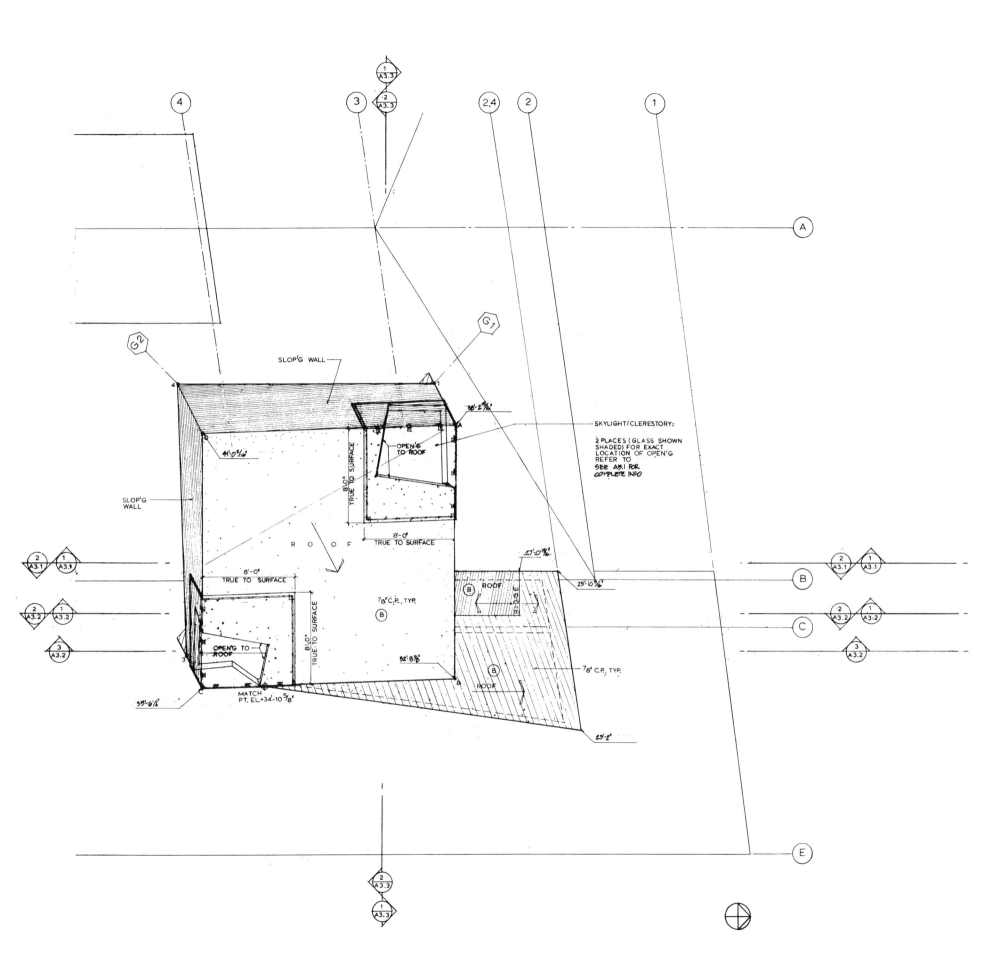

SLOP'G WALL

SLOP'G WALL

G2

G1

OPEN'G TO ROOF

SKYLIGHT/CLERESTORY:

2 PLACES (GLASS SHOWN SHADED) FOR EXACT LOCATION OF OPEN'G REFER TO
SEE A3.1 FOR COMPLETE INFO

R O O F

41'-0 5/16"

8'-0" TRUE TO SURFACE

8'-0" TRUE TO SURFACE

8'-0" TRUE TO SURFACE

8'-0" TRUE TO SURFACE

36'-2 7/8"

7 8" C.P., TYP.

B

B

ROOF

B

RIDGE

27'-0 13/16"

25'-10 3/4"

OPEN'G TO ROOF

MATCH PT. EL.+34-10 5/8"

35'-6 1/4"

32'-8 7/8"

B

ROOF

7 8" C.P., TYP.

25'-2"

CONSTRUCTION DOCUMENT *Roof Plan* SCALE 1/8"=1-0'

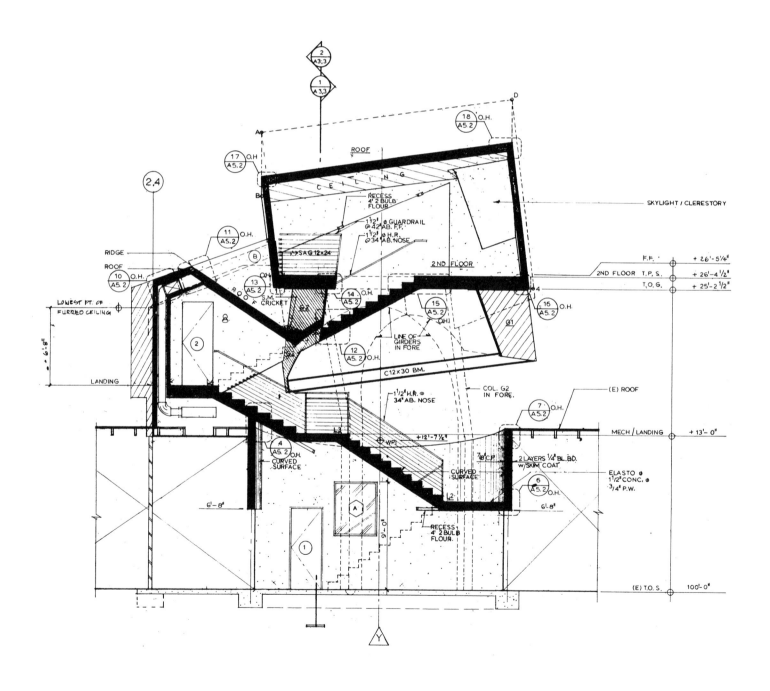

CONSTRUCTION DOCUMENT *Section* 2/A3.2 SCALE 1/8"=1-0'

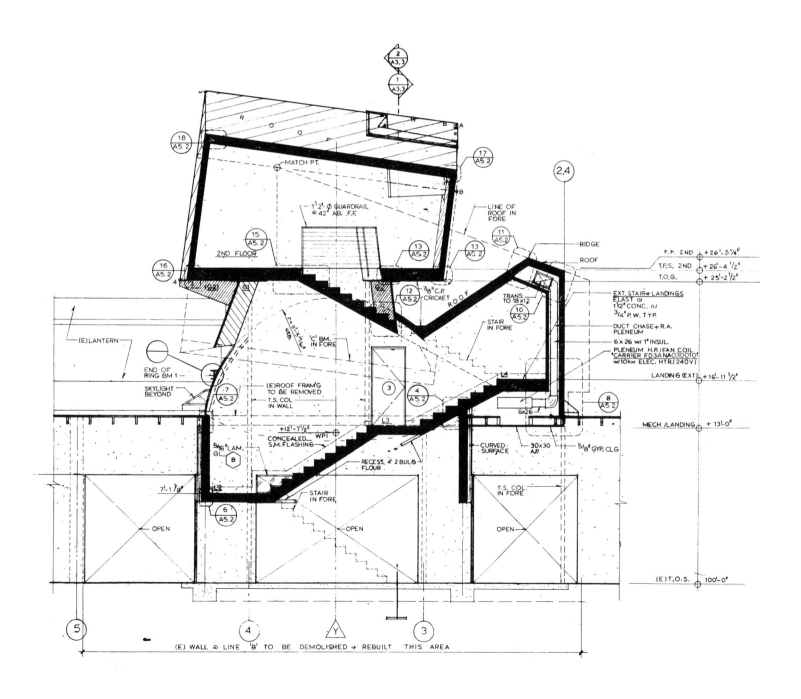

CONSTRUCTION DOCUMENT *Section* 1/A3.2 SCALE 1/8"=1-0'

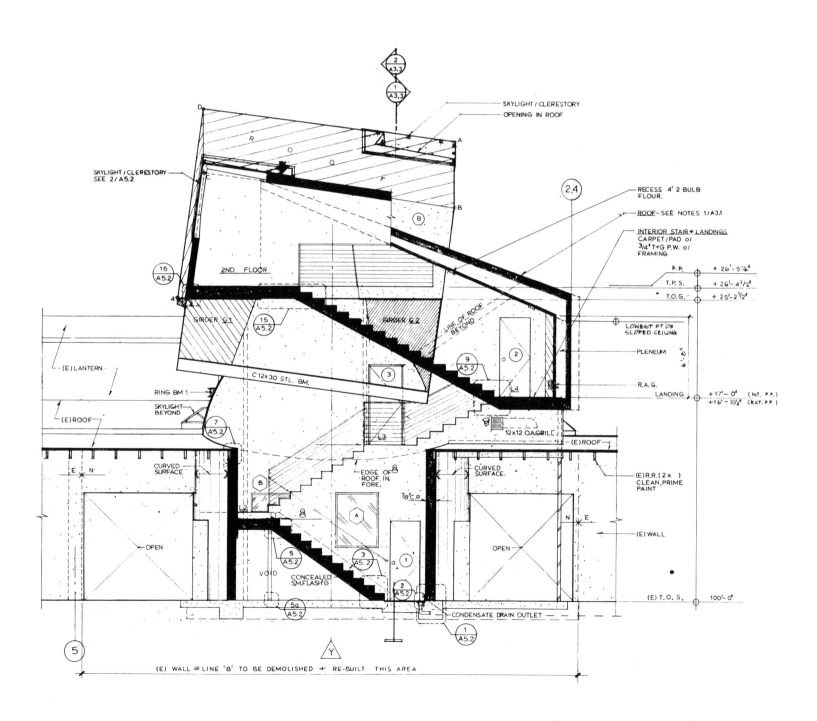

SKYLIGHT / CLERESTORY

OPENING IN ROOF

SKYLIGHT / CLERESTORY
SEE 2/A5.2

RECESS 4' 2 BULB
FLOUR.

ROOF-SEE NOTES 1/A3.1

INTERIOR STAIR & LANDINGS
CARPET / PAD o/
3/4" T+G P.W. o/
FRAMING

F.F.   + 26'- 5¼"
T.P.S.   + 26'- 4½"
T.O.G.   + 25'-2½"

2ND FLOOR

16
A5.2

GIRDER G1

15
A5.2

GIRDER G.2

LINE OF ROOF
BEYOND

LOWEST PT OF
SLOPED CEILING

PLENEUM

9
A5.2

2

B

R.A.G.

LANDING   + 17'- 0"   (INT. F.F.)
              + 16'- 11½" (EXT. F.F.)

C 12x30 STL. BM.

3

(E) LANTERN

RING BM 1

SKYLIGHT
BEYOND

7
A5.2

(E) ROOF

L3

12 x 12 O.A.GRILL

(E) ROOF

EDGE OF
ROOF. IN
FORE.

7/8" C.P.

CURVED
SURFACE

E N

B

CURVED
SURFACE.

(E) R.R. (2x)
CLEAN, PRIME
PAINT

L2

A

N   E

(E) WALL

OPEN

5
A5.2

3
A5.2

1

OPEN

VOID

CONCEALED
S.M.FLASH'G

2
A5.2

(E) T.O.S.   100'- 0"

5a
A5.2

CONDENSATE DRAIN OUTLET

1
A5.2

5

Y

(E) WALL @ LINE 'B' TO BE DEMOLISHED + RE-BUILT THIS AREA

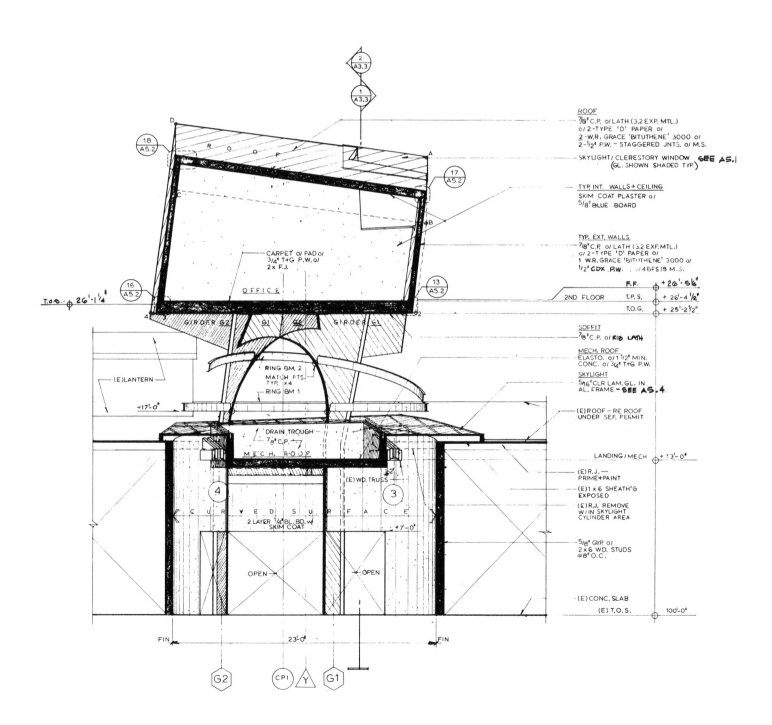

ROOF
7/8" C.P. o/ LATH (3.2 EXP. MTL.)
o/ 2-TYPE 'D' PAPER o/
2-W.R. GRACE 'BITUTHENE' 3000 o/
2-1/2" P.W. – STAGGERED JNTS. o/ M.S.

SKYLIGHT/ CLERESTORY WINDOW **SEE A5.1**
(GL. SHOWN SHADED TYP.)

TYP. INT. WALLS + CEILING
SKIM COAT PLASTER o/
5/8" BLUE BOARD

TYP. EXT. WALLS
7/8" C.P. o/ LATH (3.2 EXP. MTL.)
o/ 2-TYPE 'D' PAPER o/
1 W.R. GRACE 'BITUTHENE' 3000 o/
1/2" CDX P.W. o/ 4 BF SJ9 M.S.

F.F.   + 26'-5 1/2"
2ND FLOOR   T.P.S.   + 26'-4 1/2"
             T.O.G.   + 25'-2 1/2"

SOFFIT
7/8" C.P. o/ RIB LATH

MECH. ROOF
ELASTO. o/ 1 1/2" MIN.
CONC. o/ 3/4" T+G P.W.

SKYLIGHT
5/16" CLR LAM. GL. IN
AL. FRAME **SEE A5.4**

(E) ROOF – RE ROOF
UNDER SEP. PERMIT

LANDING / MECH   + 13'-0"

(E) R.J. –
PRIME + PAINT

(E) 1 x 6 SHEATH'G
EXPOSED

(E) R.J. REMOVE
W/IN SKYLIGHT
CYLINDER AREA

5/8" GYP. o/
2 x 6 WD. STUDS
@ 8" O.C.

(E) CONC. SLAB
(E) T.O.S.   100'-0"

CONSTRUCTION DOCUMENT *Section* 1/A3.1 SCALE 1/8"=1-0'

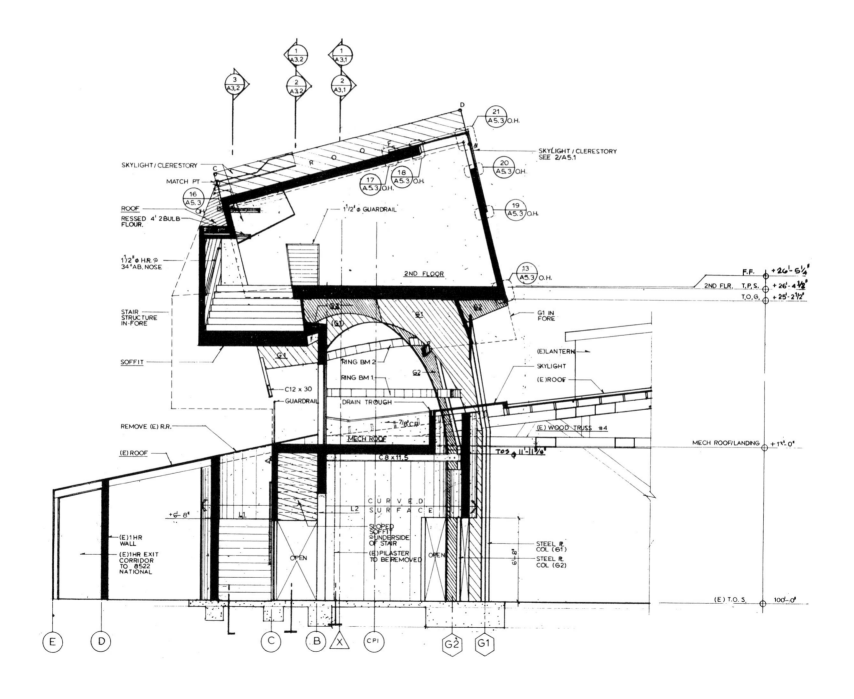

SKYLIGHT / CLERESTORY

MATCH PT

ROOF
RESSED 4' 2 BULB
FLOUR.

1½" Ø H.R. @
34" AB. NOSE

STAIR
STRUCTURE
IN-FORE

SOFFIT

C12 × 30

GUARDRAIL

REMOVE (E) R.R.

(E) ROOF

(E) 1HR
WALL

(E) 1HR EXIT
CORRIDOR
TO 8522
NATIONAL

16
A5.3

1½" Ø GUARDRAIL

17
A5.3 O.H.

18
A5.3 O.H.

2ND FLOOR

G1

(G1)

G1

RING BM 2

RING BM 1

G2

DRAIN TROUGH

⅞"CB

MECH ROOF

C8 × 11.5

+6'-8"

L1

L2

CURVED
SURFACE

SLOPED
SOFFIT @
UNDERSIDE
OF STAIR

(E) PILASTER
TO BE REMOVED

OPEN

OPEN

21
A5.3 O.H.

20
A5.3 O.H.

SKYLIGHT / CLERESTORY
SEE 2/A5.1

19
A5.3 O.H.

13
A5.3 O.H.

G1 IN
FORE

(E) LANTERN

SKYLIGHT

(E) ROOF

(E) WOOD TRUSS #4

TOS 11'-11½"

STEEL P.
COL (G1)

STEEL P.
COL (G2)

6'-8"

F.F. +26'-6¼"
2ND FLR. T.P.S. +26'-4½"
T.O.G. +25'-2½"

MECH ROOF/LANDING +12'-0"

(E) T.O.S. 100'-0"

E   D   C   B   X   CP1   G2   G1

3
A3,2

2
A3,2

1
A3,2

2
A3,1

1
A3,1

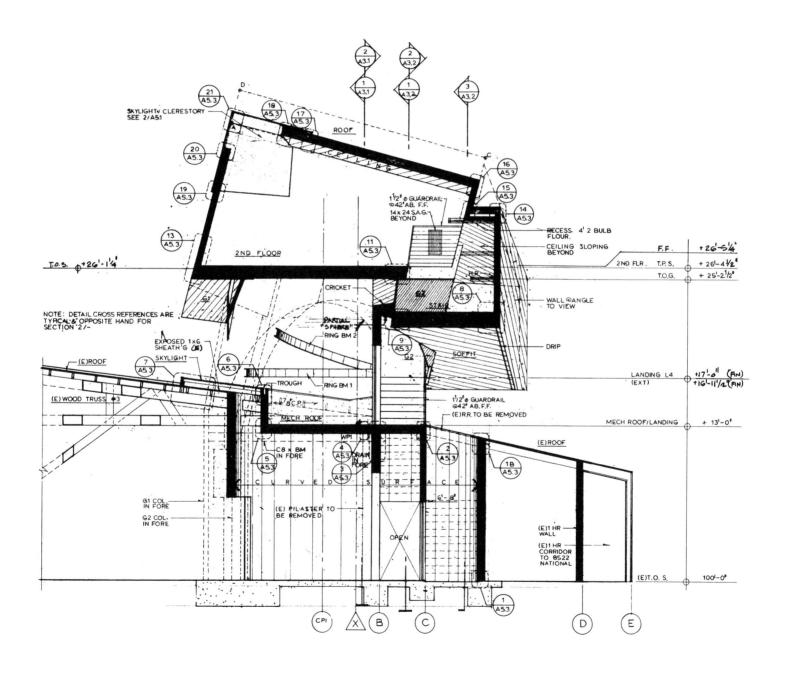

NOTE: DETAIL CROSS REFERENCES ARE
TYPICAL & OPPOSITE HAND FOR
SECTION '2/-

CONSTRUCTION DOCUMENT *Section* 1/A3.3 SCALE 1/8"=1-0'

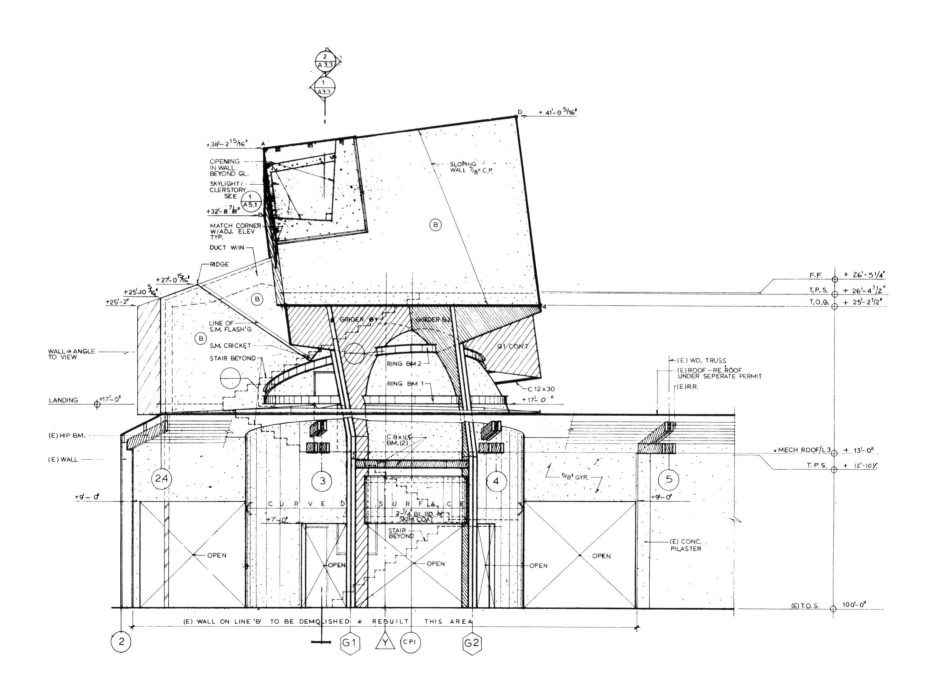

CONSTRUCTION DOCUMENT *West Elevation* SCALE 1/8"=1-0'

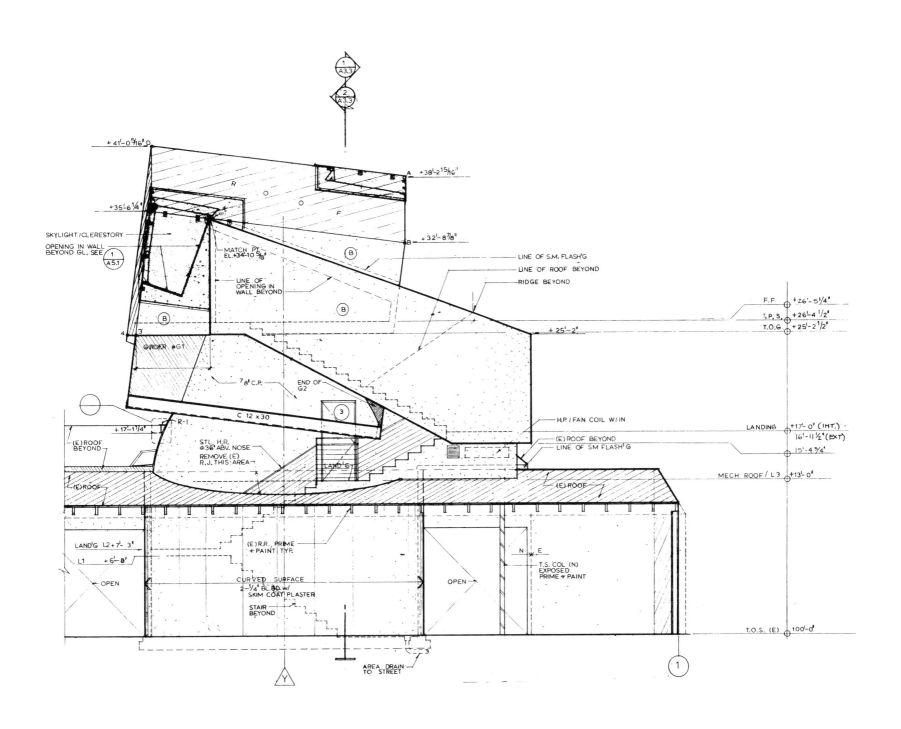

CONSTRUCTION DOCUMENT *East Elevation* SCALE 1/8"=1-0'

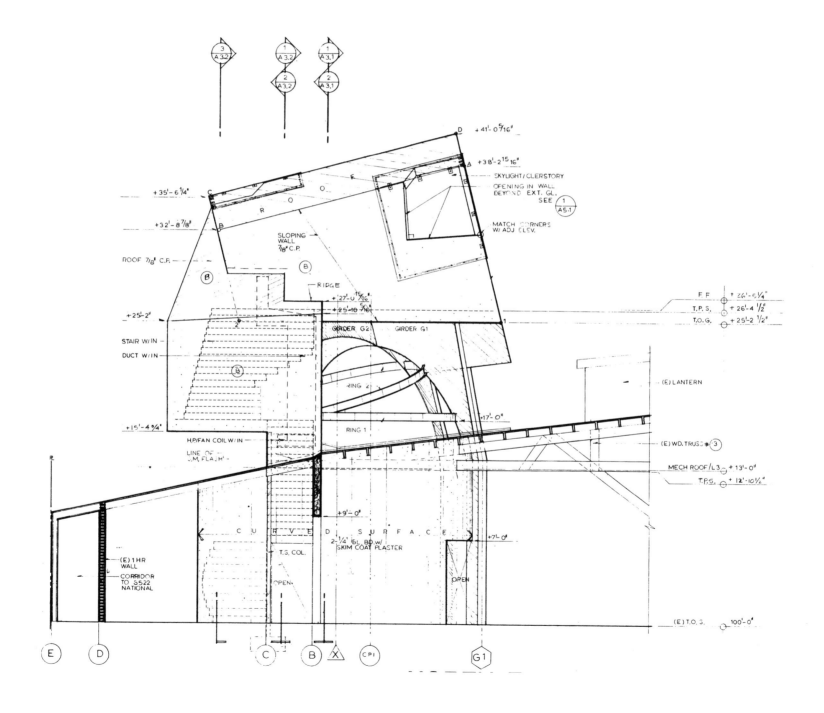

CONSTRUCTION DOCUMENT *North Elevation* SCALE 1/8"=1-0'

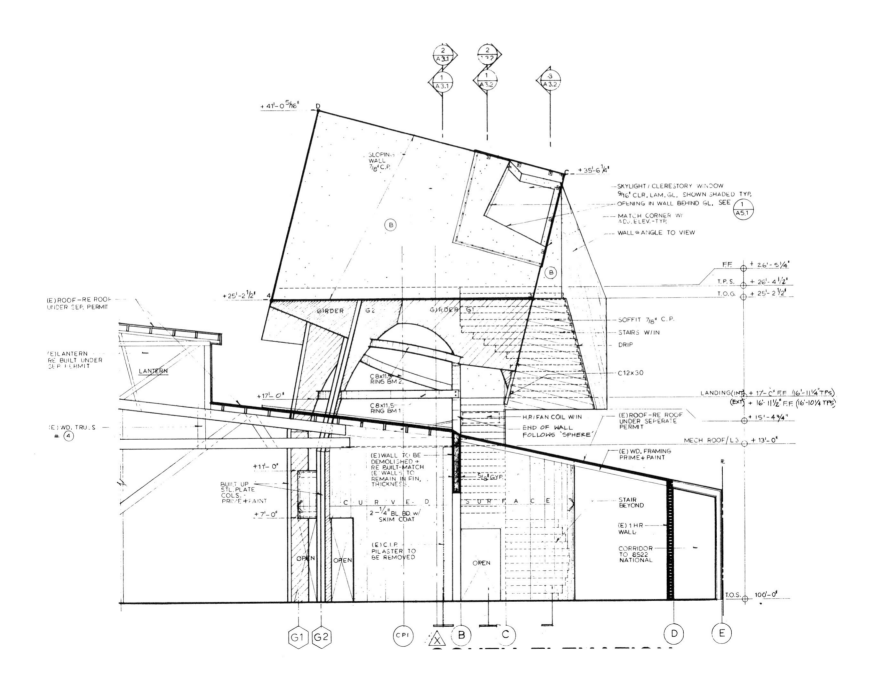

When Eric Moss approached me about working with him on a book I was skeptical at first. Not because the work isn't interesting, but because this is a request I often get from architects. What would make this book worth doing? What would make it jump out from a bookstore's shelves? What would make it different from the monographs already published on his work?

The more I talked with Eric the more interested I became in taking on a book project with him. A voracious reader, his conversations are peppered with references to Nietsche, Kierkegaard, Kurosawa, Robert Hughes, and to his late father, the writer and poet Moss Herbert. Sitting down for a cup of coffee with Eric is never a dull experience but rather an engaging, challenging one. Sometimes I thought that agreeing to do this project, and persuading the GSD to support it, was like accepting a dare from Eric. Would I be able to work with him–cantankerous and infuriating as he can be at times? Would I be able to choose the right voices, the right photographer, the right designer to communicate the qualities of Eric's work that make it so exhilarating?

Through a fairly long involvement with exhibitions and publications of architecture, I have become interested in exploring issues related to the representation of this three-dimensional art in different media. Exhibitions of architecture can never exhibit their subject matter, only representations of it. Publications can be filled with beautiful photographs that nevertheless fail to communicate such important aspects of a building as the tactility of the materials, the sensation of moving through its spaces, climbing its stairs, looking out to views framed by its openings, and experiencing the effects caused by shifts in light from dusk to dawn.

This book, on one of Eric Moss's most recent Culver City projects, The Box, is the third in a series of GSD publications on a single building. It is supported by the School's Eliot Noyes Visiting Design Critic Fund, a position Eric held in the spring of 1993. With this publication, I hope to give the reader a sense of what it is like to be in one of Eric's buildings. For, after walking through all the Culver City projects with Eric in January 1994, I realized that his work is incredibly difficult to photograph. In fact, it is almost impossible to imagine what it is like to be in these buildings, the richness of the materials, or the satisfaction one experiences on turning a corner or entering a room and encountering one of Eric's witty gestures, just by looking at photographs. Consequently, I have looked to other ways by which to communicate the essence of The Box.

From start to finish it has been a challenge to convince Eric of the aptness and the skill of the various contributors I wanted him to work with. For someone whose work is tough and edgy, I was surprised when he was not immediately receptive to my suggestions of photographer, designer, and interviewer and instead suggested that we work with people with whom he was already familiar. So, in a way, I issued my own dare to Eric by stubbornly insisting that he at least try working with those I recommended. In the end, the struggle was well worth it as, in all cases, Eric had to admit that the choices were right.

The interview with Eric by Scott Cohen is probing and dense. Scott asks difficult questions about the thought process,

the influences, and inspirations, and in doing so allows us to grasp something of the mental process and struggle

and the incredibly complex machinations behind the work.

Andrew Bush was commissioned to photograph The Box even though his photographic work does not normally

extend to architecture. By asking an artist rather than a documenter to photograph the building, we have

gained photographs that are interpretive and elegant and that are, Eric admits, among the most incisive

photographs ever taken of his work. Through the sequencing of Bush's photographs we have tried to

give the sense of moving through the building.

And working with the book's designer, Anita Meyer, we have tried to give the book some of the

tactility, some of the toughness, and some of the guts of Eric Moss's work.

In the end, both Eric and I agree that making this book was a challenge worth accepting.

Scott Cohen is an Associate Professor of Architecture at Harvard University Graduate School of Design. Since 1987, Cohen's practice has included houses and interiors in Texas, New York, New Jersey, and Florida, and numerous speculative projects. Presently, his practice and research focus on redeploying descriptive geometry as a method with which to permute architectural form. His work has been published in *Architectural Design*, *AA Files*, *Assemblage*, *AppendX* and *Harvard Architectural Review*.

Brooke Hodge is Director of Lectures, Exhibitions, and Academic Publications at the Graduate School of Design where she teaches a seminar on issues of architectural representation. She was Exhibitions Coordinator at the Canadian Centre for Architecture from 1985–1991 and in 1991 she was appointed Commissioner for the Canadian Pavilion at the Fifth International Exhibition of Architecture at the Venice Biennale.

Peter G. Rowe is Raymond Garbe Professor of Architecture and Urban Design and Dean at the Graduate School of Design, Harvard University. He is the author of *Modernity and Housing* (1993), *Making a Middle Landscape* (1991), *Design Thinking* (1987), and coauthor of *Principles for Local Environmental Management* (1978).

Herbert Muschamp is the architecture critic for *The New York Times* and the author of *File Under Architecture* (1974), *Man About Town: Frank Lloyd Wright in New York City* (1983), and T*he Once and Future Park* (1993).

Andrew Bush is a photographer who lives in Los Angeles. His photographs of people in their cars, envelopes, x-rays, among other subjects, have been exhibited and are included in the collections of many galleries and museums in the United States and abroad. He is also the author of *Bonnettstown, a house in Ireland* (1989).

Mack Scogin is Kajima Adjunct Professor of Architecture at the Graduate School of Design, where he was Chairman of the department of Architecture from 1990–1995. He is a principal in the Atlanta firm of Scogin Elam and Bray Architects.

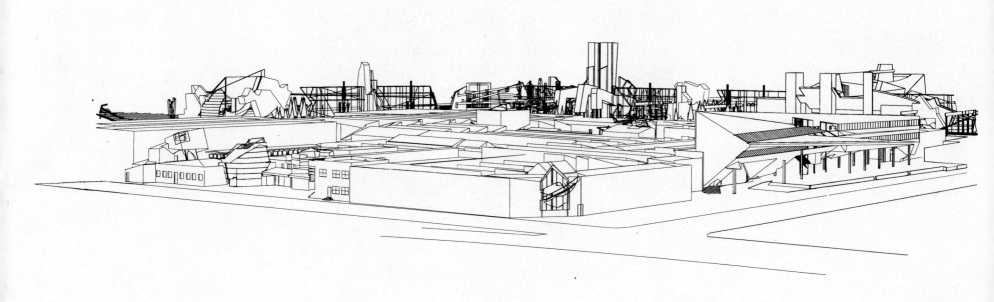

THE BOX *Credits*

OWNER	Frederick Norton Smith
ARCHITECT	Eric Owen Moss
PROJECT ARCHITECT	Jay Vanos
PROJECT TEAM	Lucas Rios
	Scott Nakao
	Scott Hunter
	Eric Stultz
	Todd Conversano
	Sheng-yuan Hwang
	Paul Groh
	Thomas Ahn
GENERAL CONTRACTOR	Peter Brown, Superintendent
	Samitaur Constructs
	Culver City, California
STRUCTURAL ENGINEER	Joe Kurily
	Kurily, Syzmansky, Tchircow, Inc.
	Santa Monica, California
ELECTRICAL ENGINEERS	John Snyder
	John Snyder and Associates
	Burbank, California

Eric would like to thank Frederick and Laurie Smith,
Jay Vanos, Peter Brown, and Lucas Rios.

THE BOX *General Specifications*

STRUCTURAL SYSTEM	Built-Up Steel Frame
EXTERIOR CLADDING	Custom System Glass
	by Morse Sheet Metal
	Exterior Cement Plaster
	over Metal Studs
ROOF	
ELASTOMETRIC	Membrane Waterproofing
	Bituthene by W.R. Grace
	Deck Coating *Excel-Coat*
	by Excellent Coating
	Built-Up Roofing by Manville
GLASS	Custom System manufactured
	by Morse Sheet Metal
TEMPERED GLASS	1/2" clear Downey Glass
LAMINATED GLASS	9/16" clear by Glass Pro
HARDWARE	Full Mortise by Schlage
CLOSERS	Floor by Dorma
INTERIOR FINISHES	
SPECIAL COATINGS	Exterior Portland Cement Plaster
	by California Stucco
	Eddie Castillo Plaster
CARPET	*Woolgrain* pattern #142
	by Carousel Carpets,
	Eureka, California
LIGHTING FIXTURES	
INDOOR	Custom by Westco Electric
OUTDOOR	Floods and Spots by Stonco

ERIC OWEN MOSS

BORN   July 25, 1943, Los Angeles, California

EDUCATED   University of California at Los Angeles, Bachelor of Arts, 1965

                        University of California at Berkeley, College of Environmental Design, Master of Architecture with Honors, 1968

                        Harvard University, Graduate School of Design, Master of Architecture, 1972

ESTABLISHED   Eric Owen Moss Architects, 1976

AWARDS   AIA/Los Angeles Design Award, 1992

                        National AIA Interior Design Awards of Excellence (2), 1992

                        Progressive Architecture Design Awards (2), 1992

                        AIA/Los Angeles Honor Awards (2), 1991

                        AIA/California Council Urban Design Award, 1991

ACADEMIC AFFILIATIONS   Professor of Design and Member of Board of Directors,

                        Southern California Institute of Architecture, Los Angeles, California, on-going

                        Eliot Noyes Chair, Harvard University, Graduate School of Design,

                        Cambridge, Massachusetts, 1993

                        Eero Saarinen Chair, Yale University, New Haven, Connecticut, 1991

                        Harvard University, Graduate School of Design, Cambridge, Massachusetts, 1990

                        Columbia University, Graduate School of Architecture and Urban Planning,

                        New York, New York, 1986

PROFESSIONAL AFFILIATIONS College of Fellows, American Institute of Architects, 1992

EXHIBITIONS   Aspen Art Museum, Current work, Aspen, Colorado, June 3 through July 4, 1993

                        Harvard University, Graduate School of Design, Current work, Cambridge, Massachusetts, Spring 1993

                        Progressive Architecture "New Public Realm" touring exhibition:

                        Washington, D.C., New York, Toronto, Denver, San Francisco, Los Angeles, October 1992 through April 1993

                        65 Thompson Street, Gagosian Castelli Gallery, "Angels and Franciscans:

                        Innovative Architecture from Los Angeles and San Francisco,"

                        New York, New York, September 26 through November 7, 1992,

                        tours to the Santa Monica Museum of Art, Santa Monica, California, February 7 through March 1993

                        Architectural Design "Theory and Experimentation," Symposium/Exhibition, London, England, June 1992

SELECTED BUILDINGS AND PROJECTS *Eric Owen Moss Architects*

1995	Gasometer (The Tank), Vienna, Austria	in design
	Vesey Street Turnaround, Battery Park City, New York	in design
	Nueva Vieja Nueva Vieja, Havana, Cuba	in design
	A.R. City, Los Angeles, California	in design
1994	Samitaur II, Los Angeles, California	project
	Callig Wien, Wagramerstrasse, Vienna, Austria	project
	Ince Theater, Culver City, California	project
	3535 Hayden Avenue, Culver City, California	under construction
	3R Theatre, Culver City, California	project
	Beehive, Culver City, California	project
1993	Santa Monica Science Center, Santa Monica, California	project
	Sun Foundation (Very Large Array), Santa Fe, New Mexico	project
	I.R.S., Culver City, California	completed 1994
	Contemporary Art Center and Theater, Tours, France	competition
1992	Ibiza Paseo Commercial Center, Ibiza, Spain	project
	Stealth, Culver City, California	project
1991	Metafor, Culver City, California	completed 1995
	Hayden Tower, Culver City, California	project
	Aronoff House, Tarzana, California	project
	Nara Convention Center, Nara, Japan	competition
1990	S.P.A.R.CITY, Culver City, California	project
	The Box, Culver City, California	completed 1994
1989	Sandpiper Bridge, Culver City, California	project
	Samitaur I, Los Angeles, California	completed 1996
	Wedgewood Holly Complex, Culver City, California	project
1988	Lawson/Westen House, Los Angeles, California	completed 1993
	Gary Group Office Building, Culver City, California	completed 1990
1987	Paramount Laundry Office Building, Culver City, California	completed 1989
	Lindblade Tower, Culver City, California	completed 1989
1986	8522 National Office Complex, Culver City, California	all phases complete by 1992
1985	Central Housing Office Building, University of California at Irvine, Irvine, California	completed 1986

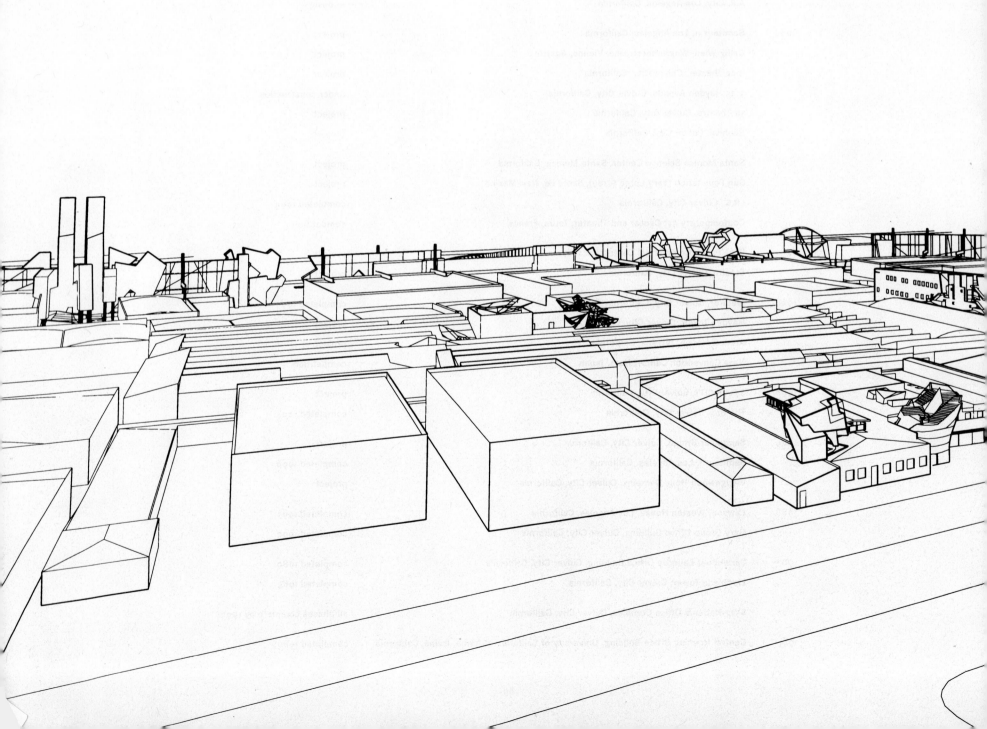

DIRECTOR OF LECTURES, EXHIBITIONS AND ACADEMIC PUBLICATIONS	Brooke Hodge
DESIGNER	Anita Meyer, plus design inc., Boston
EDITOR	Brooke Hodge
PRODUCTION COORDINATOR	Susan McNally, Cambridge
PROJECT ASSISTANTS	Tamara Gould and Raymond Ricord, Eric Owen Moss Architects
SCANS	Jay Berman
PHOTOGRAPHY CREDITS	page 20 (bottom) Paul Aroh
	pages 15, 19, 20 (top), 22, 24 Todd Conversano
	page 16 Frank Jackson
	All other interview photographs courtesy of Eric Owen Moss Architects
PRINTER	Mercantile Printing Company, Worcester, Massachusetts

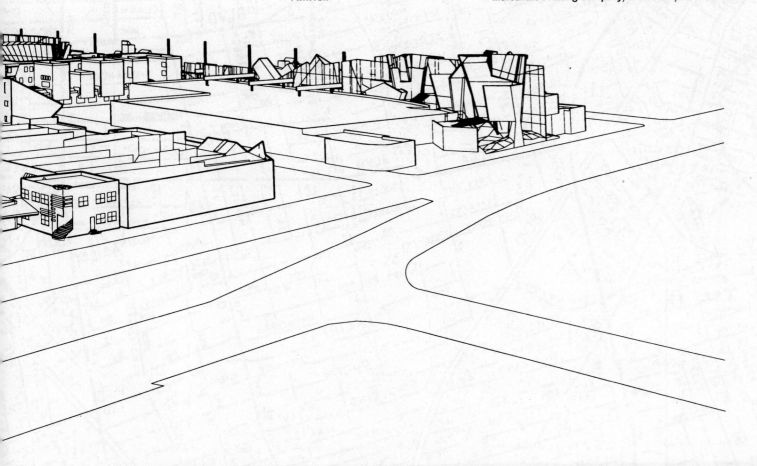